Before Buying Cybersecurity
How to Evaluate, Negotiate, and Partner with IT Security Providers

Nikolay Gul

"Clarity is the highest form of security"

ISBN (paperback): 979-8-9927440-9-5
ISBN (eBook): 979-8-9938806-0-0
Library of Congress Control Number: 2025923715

This publication is intended for educational, advisory, and informational purposes only. It does not constitute legal or cybersecurity advice. Readers should consult certified security and legal professionals for implementation decisions.

Published by **Future-Proof Marketing Press**, New York.

Printed in the United States of America

Before Buying Cybersecurity How to Evaluate, Negotiate, and Partner with IT Security Providers

Foreword
by Tush Nikollaj, President & CEO, Logical Net Corporation

In cybersecurity, trust is not a slogan, it's a measurable outcome.

Over the years leading a managed security service provider, I've sat across from hundreds of smart, capable business leaders who all asked the same question in different ways: *"How do I know I'm really protected?"*

It's a fair question, and for too long, our industry hasn't given it a clear answer. We've buried clarity under jargon, acronyms, and dashboards. Somewhere along the way, cybersecurity became more about appearances than assurance.

Every day, executives face complex threats, conflicting advice, and a marketplace full of tools that sound impressive but are difficult to evaluate. With so many voices competing for attention, clarity matters just as much as technology.

That's what makes **Before Buying Cybersecurity** such a valuable and timely book. It cuts through the noise and brings the focus back to what really matters, practical decisions and trust built on measurable outcomes. It helps readers understand what truly protects them, what questions to ask service providers, and how to choose confidently without getting lost in jargon or sales pressure.

For more than three decades, Logical Net has focused on pairing strong technical capabilities with accountability, transparency, and partnership. This book reflects those same values. Cybersecurity isn't a one-time purchase or a product, it's an ongoing relationship built on informed choices, verifiable practices, and mutual trust.

If this guide helps even one business leader or organization demand clarity, make smarter, safer, and more confident decisions, and strengthen their security posture with purpose, it will have achieved something meaningful, not just for them, but for our entire industry and community.

About the Author of the Foreword

Tush Nikollaj is the President & CEO of Logical Net Corporation, a managed IT and cybersecurity services provider based in New York. With over three decades of experience helping organizations strengthen resilience through technology, Tush advocates for clarity, measurable outcomes, and lasting partnerships in the cybersecurity industry.

Why This Book Now

Cyber risk stopped being a technical issue the moment it began bankrupting companies that were perfectly "compliant."
Boards, founders, and small-business owners now face the same question: *how do we buy protection without buying confusion?*

This book exists because clarity has become the missing product in cybersecurity.
In every breach investigation and vendor negotiation I've witnessed, the damage didn't begin with hackers—it began with misunderstanding.

You don't need another alarm bell; you need a map.
What follows is not theory but proof: practical tools, clear models, audits, and questions you can use the same day to test your partners, your policies, and your own assumptions.

If this book saves you one bad contract, one needless panic, or one sleepless night—it has done its job.
That's why this book exists now.

Clarity creates trust. Trust creates resilience.

This book respects cybersecurity partners who innovate with integrity. Its goal isn't to expose competitors but to empower collaboration built on measurable outcomes.

Nikolay Gul

Introduction — The Clarity Threshold

"If your board asked for one measurable proof of cybersecurity readiness today, could you show it in under 60 seconds? Most executives can't. This book exists to close that gap."

Why cybersecurity feels complicated — and how smart leaders make it simple

Most people buy cybersecurity like umbrellas: in a storm, at a premium, and with the hope they'll never test it. Then the storm hits—and the umbrella refuses to open. The result is familiar: shelves of dashboards, little real defense. We think we're buying technology; too often we're buying reassurance dressed as protection.

One misconception that quietly increases organizational risk is the belief that cybersecurity vendors absorb your legal responsibility during a breach. They do not. Accountability for business continuity, regulatory reporting, and customer impact always remains with the organization, even when technical execution is outsourced.

Cybersecurity isn't a product—it's a **decision system**. Decision systems fail less from carelessness than from noise: jargon, urgency, and fear that overwhelm judgment. This book begins where most contracts end—with **understanding**.

Why clarity beats fear
Fear drives panic buying. Clarity drives smart contracts, transparent partnerships, and measurable outcomes. When you understand how security works—technically, financially, and psychologically—you stop reacting and start **designing**.

A 60-Second Audit
Rate each 1–5 (strongly disagree → strongly agree):

1. I can explain what my provider does in one sentence my board understands.
2. I've seen proof they test their own systems.
3. They've admitted a past mistake—and what changed.
4. I know exactly who to call at 3 a.m. and what happens next.
5. Our SLA defines response times with numbers, not adjectives.
   Score 0–10: theater; 11–18: gaps remain; 19–25: solid—this book sharpens the edge.

The Clarity Matrix
Clarity = (Transparency × Competence × Consistency) ÷ Ego Bias

Ego Bias – Defensive posturing or jargon that erodes clarity; Clarity Matrix – (Transparency × Competence × Consistency) ÷ Ego Bias.

- *Transparency*: plain language, honest updates—good and bad.
- *Competence*: measurable results, not adjectives.
- *Consistency*: promises kept again and again.
- *Ego Bias*: defensiveness, jargon, blame. When ego rises, clarity collapses.

Five micro-tests before you sign

- Three references with **measurable outcomes**.
- A **150-word explainer** your board will understand.
- Six months of **SLA (Service Level Agreement** data) wins and misses.
- A **tabletop drill** outline: who acts, when, with what authority.
- **One mistake** they owned—and what changed.
  These five questions expose vague scope, weak follow-through, and "green-dashboard" illusions in minutes.

How to use this book
Each chapter opens with a quick audit, moves through field-tested tools and models (for example, the Clarity Matrix and Trust Equation), and closes with a Key Summary plus a short Closing Reflection. You can read straight through for a full blueprint or jump directly to the

chapter that matches today's decision. Either way, you finish with outcomes you can verify, not just ideas you can admire.

Who this book is for

- Executives tired of green dashboards that hide red risks.
- IT leaders caught between compliance checklists and real threats.
- Founders and SMB owners who want confidence before contracts.
- Cybersecurity vendors committed to selling ethically and intelligently.
  If you've ever signed a contract you didn't fully understand—or nodded through a meeting where "quantum XDR" sounded more magical than practical—this book will decode it.

Why This Book Helps Both Sides of the Table

One of the goals of this book is to strengthen—not divide—the relationship between cybersecurity providers and the business leaders they serve. Ethical vendors, MSPs, and security professionals work hard to deliver clarity, but the language gap between technical teams and business leadership often creates misunderstanding on both sides.

This book offers a shared vocabulary of trust.
It gives buyers a clearer way to understand what they are being offered, and it gives providers a framework to present their services in the language that SMB owners and executives use to make decisions.

If you are a cybersecurity professional or MSP leader, this book helps you win more deals with less friction. If you are the buyer, it helps you choose partners who match your expectations and your values.

This book builds on the foundation introduced in my earlier work, AI-Driven Cybersecurity & High-Tech Marketing, advancing the conversation from understanding cybersecurity to buying it with clarity, confidence, and measurable accountability.

My promise to you
No blind trust. Every framework here is verifiable. Every statistic and example comes from current, transparent, public data. I will respect your intelligence and challenge your assumptions. By the final page, you won't wonder, *"Is our security good enough?"*—you'll know how to measure it yourself.

When buyers understand cybersecurity better, ethical providers sell more effectively, renewals improve, and partnerships strengthen. Clarity serves everyone.
Every chapter ends with an audit, prompt, or checklist you can use the same day.

Welcome to the Clarity Threshold where cybersecurity stops being a mystery and becomes a mindset.

PART I — THE PSYCHOLOGY OF CYBER BUYING
Quick-Start Map
Five Critical Questions to Ask Any Provider

1. What exactly will you monitor 24/7, and what won't you?
2. Who owns incident response when something goes wrong?
3. What is your guaranteed detection time and response time?
4. How do you prove your work every month?
5. What happens if your tools fail?

Three Red Flags
- No written response-time guarantees
- No monthly reporting or evidence
- Blaming "the vendor" for gaps instead of taking accountability

Three Vendor Types (Know Which One You're Buying)
- **Tool Resellers** — sell licenses, little support
- **MSPs** — support IT, limited security depth
- **MSSPs/SOCs** — actual security operations

Budget Snapshot
Spend **70% on people and process, 30% on tools** — not the other way around.

Your Fast Due-Diligence Checklist
- Confirm 24/7 coverage
- Verify SLAs in writing
- Ask for sample incident reports
- Request 3 customer references
- Validate who presses the "panic button" at 3 AM

If you read only this page, you already reduce your risk more than most companies ever do.

Chapter 1: The Trust Gap

Why Cybersecurity Feels Risky and How to Choose Wisely

Before you buy cybersecurity, pause. Most regrets start before the paperwork.

The biggest risk isn't the one you can't see - it's the one you trust without proof.

The Call That Sounded Familiar

Early one Thursday morning, **Emily Porter**, deputy director of procurement for a contractor serving the **U.S. Department of Agriculture**, prepared for a routine vendor audit.
A voicemail appeared from her boss, the regional director:
"Process that supplier payment right away—our inspection sites can't lose refrigeration."
The voice was flawless. Same rhythm, same mild impatience, even the faint office hum she'd heard on countless calls.

Within fifteen minutes she released a **$247,800 ACH transfer** to the "temporary cold-storage vendor."
By noon, the real vendor called—no payment received.
IT reviewed the logs: no breach, no alerts, every control green.
The voicemail had been generated by **AI voice-cloning software** trained on ten minutes of public webcast audio.
The confirming email came from a **spoofed domain** differing by one character.
The money vanished through layered crypto wallets before lunch.

The FBI later traced more than **$10 million** in similar thefts that quarter across multiple agencies and suppliers.

Emily's case became one of the first American examples of what investigators now call *"The Year of Synthetic Trust."*

Why Trust Feels Risky

Attacks like this don't exploit technology; they exploit recognition.
Humans are wired to respond faster to voices we know.
Every organization teaches people to doubt strangers, yet few teach them to verify friends.
That reflex—automatic confidence in the familiar—is the hidden fault line running through every modern network.

When executives say cybersecurity "feels risky," they're describing this emotional mismatch.
Dashboards show perfection, but intuition whispers otherwise.
It isn't paranoia; it's the mind noticing that assurance has outpaced evidence.

The Board Snap-Test — A Two-Minute Reality Check

At your next leadership meeting, ask aloud:

• What promise did our provider make last quarter that we cannot prove was kept?
  • What actually changed after the last incident report?
  • Where is that change documented?

Three honest answers reveal your trust gap.
If all three exist in writing, you own clarity.
If not, you own risk.
This simple exercise turns the Clarity Matrix from theory into board-visible behavior.

The U.S.-Scale Problem

According to the **FBI Internet Crime Report 2024,** Americans lost over **$3.5 billion** to business-email and voice-impersonation fraud—three times the 2021 figure.
In agriculture and logistics alone, deep-voice scams cost more than **$120 million**, often wrapped in urgent operational language designed to short-circuit reason.

The losses are measurable; the hesitation they create is not.
Each false signal slows a genuine decision.
Every doubt between partners becomes another invoice delayed, another protective policy unsigned.
Mistrust accumulates interest faster than any ransom demand.

"The synthetic trust attack on Emily (via voice clone) succeeded because the denominator of trust—Assumption—was maxed out. Our updated Trust Equation 2.0 mandates continuous Verification, which synthetic attacks cannot fake."

A **CISO** (Chief Information Security Officer) once told me something I never forgot: "The first moment of doubt is the most expensive piece of human-layer security you already own. Don't dismiss it — investigate it. That small whisper that something feels 'off' is your first alert system, and it's the only one attackers can't disable."

Closing the Trust Gap

1. **Prove voices with protocol.**
   Any transfer above a threshold requires a callback to a verified number—never the one in the request.

2. **Log the human layer.**

    Record each exception and its approval trail; auditors and insurers will demand it later.

3. **Score conversations, not just controls.**

    If a decision isn't documented, it isn't secured.

4. **Run the 60-Second Audit.**

    Once a quarter, time how long it takes your team to prove a promise was kept.

    If it takes more than sixty seconds, your clarity is running slower than your risk.

Genius Tip: The CEO's 5-Second Test

Before approving any cybersecurity renewal or new contract, ask your IT leader:

"If this core service disappeared tomorrow, what exact minute does our business stop operating?"

If they cannot answer in five seconds with a specific **RTO** – Recovery Time Objective number, the risk dependency is unmeasured and the decision is premature.

Real Life Story

A **CIO** once told me something I never forgot. During a renewal meeting, the vendor kept repeating that their tool would "reduce risk by 92%." The CIO paused, looked at me, and whispered, "Ninety-two percent of what? I can't even name the risks they're measuring."

Later, when we unpacked the claim, the number came from a marketing slide—not an operational metric.

He leaned back and said, "So the real risk wasn't the tool. It was me almost trusting a number I didn't understand."

That single moment reshaped his entire buying approach. Trust didn't disappear. It matured.

If your board asked for one measurable proof of cybersecurity today, could you show it in under 60 seconds?

The 60-Second Clarity Audit

Rate 1 (strongly disagree) to 5 (strongly agree):

□ I can explain what my security provider does in one clear sentence.

□ I have seen proof they regularly test their own systems.

□ They have admitted a past mistake and shown how they fixed it.

□ I know exactly who to call at 3 a.m. if we're breached —with a direct number.

□ Our contract specifies exact response times, not vague words like "prompt."

Your score: _____ / 25

0–10 High risk → you're paying for security theater.
11–18 Partial clarity → meaningful gaps remain.
19–25 Strong foundation → this chapter sharpens your edge.

Keep this score; you'll test it again once clarity becomes measurable.

Proof in Practice – Avoiding a Trust Trap:
A Seattle non-profit ran the 60-Second Clarity Audit quarterly. When their incumbent vendor scored 23/25, they confidently renewed. A flashy competitor scored only 11/25 (defensive answers, unclear

proof), so they walked away saving an estimated $180,000 in 3 years. **Clarity prevented a costly mistake before contracts were signed.**

From Illusion to Evidence

Emily's team recovered only a fraction of the stolen funds, but the loss forced a transformation.
Every purchase order now requires dual authorization.
Voicemail attachments route through automated forensic screening.
The CFO tracks **trust metrics** beside uptime and budget.
Embarrassment became architecture.
Cybersecurity fails when clarity collapses.
The louder the alert, the easier it is to believe it's working.
Real safety begins when verification becomes reflex—when partners value your trust more than your transaction.

A CISO once told me something I never forgot: 'The first moment of doubt is the most expensive piece of human-layer security you already own. Don't dismiss it — investigate it. That whisper that something feels off is your first alert system, and it's the only one attackers can't disable.'

Chapter 2 — The Cost of Confusion

What Businesses Really Pay for Cybersecurity Mistakes

Confusion is the most expensive line item on your security budget — and it never appears on an invoice.

Breaches cost money.
  Tools cost money.
  Vendors cost money.

But misunderstanding — the silent force behind most poor security decisions — drains far more than anything attackers could steal.

This chapter reveals confusion for what it really is: an invisible financial leak, a risk multiplier, and the primary reason cybersecurity investments fail to deliver.

Once you understand the **Cost of Confusion**, every chapter after this becomes easier, sharper, and more profitable for your business.

The 60-Second Risk Budget Audit

Rate each statement from 1 (strongly disagree) to 5 (strongly agree):

1. I can list every security tool or service our organization pays for.
2. I know which of those tools are actually used each month.
3. I can tie every invoice to a specific outcome (e.g., reduced downtime, faster recovery).
4. If our provider vanished tomorrow, we could pivot within 24 hours.
5. Every tool we own is monitored by someone accountable — not by "the system."

Your Score / 25

- **0–10** → **Financial fog zone** — money quietly leaking.
- **11–18** → **Partial visibility** — you see the spend, not the results.
- **19–25** → **Operational clarity** — solid footing; more budget can still be recovered.

This audit reveals one truth: your cybersecurity budget is never what you think it is.
It is a blend of clarity and confusion — and confusion is expensive.

Confusion: The Hidden Financial Drain

Cybersecurity spending is at a historic high.
So are losses.

Not because organizations underinvest,
but because they **invest blindly**.

According to IBM's 2025 report, the average breach now costs:

- **$4.44 million** globally
- **$10.2 million** in the U.S.

Yet a significant portion of losses occur **before** the breach:

- inside budgets,
- inside proposals,
- inside contracts,
- inside half-used tools,
- inside assumptions no one verifies.

Confusion creates:

- unnecessary tools
- overlapping services
- shelfware
- missed responsibilities
- incorrect assumptions
- vague deliverables
- failed deployments
- blame cycles

This is why organizations can "spend millions on cybersecurity" yet remain dangerously unprepared.

Visual Snapshot: The Security Funnel

Imagine your cybersecurity budget as a funnel:

- A **narrow funnel** represents clarity — money flowing into real protection.
- A **wide, leaky funnel** represents confusion — money spilling everywhere.

Every unclear SLA, vague proposal, or ambiguous responsibility widens the funnel.
Clarity narrows it.

This chapter narrows your funnel.

The Cost of Confusion Formula

Confusion drains money in predictable, measurable ways.
The **Cost of Confusion Formula** turns the invisible into the obvious:

1. Overlap Waste

Paying twice for the same function because different departments bought similar tools.

2. Shelfware & Idle Tools

Tools purchased but never fully deployed, tested, or used.

3. Process Inefficiencies

Wasted time and cost during incidents when roles or procedures are unclear.

4. Misaligned Expectations

Rework, change orders, and "fixes" created by unclear or incomplete statements of work.

These four sources alone consume an estimated **15–25% of a typical security budget**.

That's not speculation — that's industry-wide data.

NEW: The Cost of Confusion Estimator

A One-Page Tool to Calculate Your Hidden Losses

Answer the following.
The more "yes" responses, the more money you're losing.

1. Do we pay for tools we don't actively use or monitor?
2. Have we purchased a tool twice (overlap) in the last 3 years?

3. Does any vendor invoice contain vague terms like "protection," "monitoring," or "coverage" without KPIs?
4. Have we ever had an incident where roles were unclear?
5. Do we have features or modules we never deployed?
6. Has any project required rework because a deliverable wasn't clearly defined?
7. Do multiple people believe they "own" the same responsibility?
8. Have we renewed a vendor contract without a full review?

Your Score (0–8):

- **0–2 → Clarity advantage (excellent).**
- **3–5 → Losing 10–20% of annual security spend.**
- **6–8 → Losing 20–35% of annual budget.**

This single tool anchors the chapter financially — replacing pages of explanation with measurable clarity.

Case Study: The Two-Million-Dollar Checkbox

A company invested **$2 million** into compliance controls, tools, and audits. Everything looked perfect — on paper.

Then ransomware hit.

- Backups existed, but had never been tested.
- Runbooks existed, but no one knew their role.
- Controls existed, but were never validated.

The results:

- weeks of downtime,
- cascading operational failures,
- a leadership shakeup,

- and a CIO who later admitted:

"We had all the technology.
What we didn't have was clarity."

Compliance delivered paperwork.
Confusion delivered loss.

The Visibility Ladder

Clarity requires visibility.
Visibility eliminates confusion.

The **Visibility Ladder** shows the path:

Bottom Rung — Blind Trust

You trust marketing slides and vendor promises.

Middle Rungs — Proof, Pilots & Transparency

You require demos, pilots, references, test results

access to logs.

Top Rung — Independence & Optionality

You:

- maintain documentation
- avoid lock-ins
- test backups regularly
- verify every claim

Every step up this ladder shrinks your **Cost of Confusion**.

Putting Clarity into Practice

Here are high-impact actions that cut confusion quickly:

1. Tool Overlap Cleanout

List all tools. Remove duplicate functions. Immediate savings.

2. Unused Capability Scan

Audit tools for features you pay for but don't use.

3. Process Clarity Test

Review your last incident or drill.
   Where did confusion cost minutes or hours?

4. Expectation Alignment

Have someone explain a vendor's deliverables in plain English.
   If they can't, renegotiate or clarify.

5. Annual Contract Review

Never renew a vendor without verifying:

- outcomes
- responsibilities
- KPIs
- alignment

Each step reduces confusion — and returns money.

The Clarity Dividend

Clarity is discipline.
  It requires:

- asking direct questions,
- demanding transparency,
- aligning roles,
- and verifying everything.

The payoff is enormous:

- fewer wasted dollars,
- fewer failures,
- faster recoveries,
- stronger vendor performance,
- higher resilience,
- and a measurable reduction in risk.

The **Cost of Confusion** isn't a cost of doing business.
  It's the cost of **unclear** business

Real Life Story
A CFO told me about a cybersecurity platform they purchased during a crisis. The vendor promised "total visibility." For six months, no one realized the system wasn't collecting logs from a critical database. The CFO admitted, "We bought clarity, but we never verified it."
When the breach investigation happened, they discovered the missing data—at the worst possible moment.
He summarized it better than any consultant could:
"The most expensive part wasn't the breach. It was the six months we believed we were protected."

Closing Reflection

If there is one pattern I have seen again and again in real conversations with business owners, it is this: the budget spreadsheet always reveals the organization's anxiety level more honestly than any meeting ever does. Every unused security tool becomes a reminder of a rushed decision made under pressure.

The Cost of Confusion is not the cost of doing business; it is the cost of unclear business. When clarity improves, spending becomes predictable, smarter, and easier to justify.

Shine a light on it —
   and watch your security investments finally deliver what you've
   been paying for.

Chapter 3 — The Vendor Mind Game

How to Outsmart Pressure, Ego, and the Illusion of Expertise

Before you compare features or prices, learn to compare motives.

In cybersecurity, the hardest threat to detect isn't malware — it's persuasion.
The subtle engineering of your decisions.
The performance of confidence as competence.
The smooth delivery that feels like expertise.

Trust rarely fails during a breach.
It fails during the sales call, when certainty sounds like security.

A good vendor reduces that uncertainty.
A weak vendor amplifies it.
A great vendor invites clarity because they know it strengthens both sides.

A Note on Fairness

This chapter is not about attacking vendors. Most cybersecurity providers are ethical professionals solving real problems. The goal here is not to undermine them — it is to **empower them** by establishing a clearer, fairer playing field where transparency wins and confusion loses.

What follows will help you identify the minority who rely on ambiguity — and reward the majority who rely on proof.

When clarity replaces guesswork, both sides win.

The 60-Second Vendor Reality Check

Rate 1 (strongly disagree) to 5 (strongly agree):

1. I understand exactly how my vendor earns revenue from my account.
2. They ask about my business goals before suggesting tools.
3. Their reports clarify risk instead of amplifying fear.
4. I can explain their pricing model to my board in one clear sentence.
5. When I decline an upsell, they remain helpful instead of defensive.

Your Score / 25

• **0–10 → High-pressure zone** — you're being sold urgency, not understanding.
• **11–18 → Mixed influence** — you see part of the game but still play by their rules.
• **19–25 → Strategic buyer** — vendors respect you because you cannot be rushed.

You will measure this score again after building your **Cognitive Firewall**.

The Psychology of the Pitch

Every vendor sells reassurance.
Some earn it.
Others rehearse it.

Most people don't realize how deeply the brain responds to fluency — messages that *sound* smooth often feel more truthful than they actually are. A confident pause, a polished slide, a familiar acronym can create an illusion of expertise long before evidence enters the conversation.

This is why buzzwords work.
When someone says "military-grade," the rational mind rolls its eyes, but the emotional mind sighs with relief. It feels safe. It feels handled. It feels like someone else has already done the worrying for you.

The antidote is not cynicism. Cynicism closes doors you may want open.
The antidote is **disciplined curiosity** — the simple habit of asking for proof the way a doctor asks for lab results. You're not challenging the person; you're validating the outcome.

Disciplined curiosity also reveals something important:
ethical vendors appreciate it.
Good partners *want* to show their work. They know that clarity is how they differentiate themselves from competitors who rely on charm or vocabulary to fill the gaps.

When you shift from passive listening to active verification, you're not creating friction — you're inviting the vendor to stand out. The honest ones rise quickly. The rehearsed ones run out of runway.

Ego-Bias — The Invisible Denominator

Ego-Bias is the reflex to protect pride faster than to seek clarity.
It shows up on both sides of the table, and it is almost always unintentional.

Both sides experience it:

• It appears when a vendor's claim lacks measurable proof, and the buyer hesitates to ask for verification.
• Buyers sometimes nod along to avoid looking uninformed.
• Vendors sometimes answer too quickly to maintain momentum—not to mislead, but because pressure compresses clarity.

Every unasked question quietly increases your Cost of Confusion.

You can spot Ego-Bias early by watching for:

1. **Language density** — when jargon rises, truth drops.
2. **Social-pressure cues** — "everyone's deploying this."
3. **Emotion spikes** — urgency replacing explanation.

Humility is a security control.
Use it deliberately.
The minute both sides let go of performance and return to clarity,
negotiation shifts from a game to a conversation.

Case Study — The State Contract That Sold Itself

A Midwestern state agency issued a bid for endpoint monitoring. Two vendors qualified.

• One led with animations, urgency, and polished delivery.
• The other brought a single page mapping the agency's public risk statements to the exact controls they needed.

The board chose the show.

Within a year, the system generated 3,000 false alerts per day, burying true incidents.
The quiet vendor later won the recovery contract — using the same one-page map.

Lesson:
When presentation outpaces proof, trust your pause.

The Negotiation Bias Loop

After every pitch:

1. Emotion creates urgency.
2. Urgency drives commitment.
3. Commitment seeks justification.

Breaking the loop requires **cool-down discipline**:

• Delay decisions 24 hours.
• Review notes without slides or salespeople.
• Ask: "What did we assume without data?"

Clarity comes from the questions you ask **after** the demo — not during it.

Real Life Story
A VP of Sales once shared an encounter with a prospect who stopped him mid-presentation. The buyer said, "Everything you're saying sounds great, but none of it matches the problems we actually have." The VP later admitted to me: "I realized I was giving the pitch I knew, not the clarity they needed."
The deal wasn't lost. It became one of the best long-term partnerships they had because the moment of honesty reset the entire conversation. His lesson was simple:
"When the buyer gets clearer, the vendor gets smarter."

Framework — The Cognitive Firewall

The **Cognitive Firewall** protects your judgment when emotions run hot.

Layer 1 — Assumption Scan

Whenever you hear "fully managed," ask: "What is excluded?"

Layer 2 — Source Verification

For each claim, request documentation or third-party audit evidence.

Layer 3 — Latency Test

If an answer comes too quickly, it's rehearsed.
Pause and ask for depth.

Layer 4 — Context Isolation

Remove brand names.
Would the statement still sound impressive?

Layer 5 — Reality Verification

Ask to see it live — not in slides.

Run these layers automatically.
You'll buy systems, not stories.

Vendor Psychology Field Notes

• **Authority Effect:** Titles and certifications trigger deference — so still ask for proof.
• **Anchoring Bias:** The first price frames the rest — ask for multiple options.
• **Scarcity Trigger:** "Only two spots left." Urgency is a signal to pause.
• **Social Proof Mirage:** Big logos prove budget, not fit.

Psychological triggers work because they sound reasonable.
Reason is your countermeasure.

Ask This, Not That — Vendor Edition

Instead of: "Do you offer 24/7 monitoring?"
Ask: "Who is awake at 2 a.m., and what authority do they have?"

Instead of: "Are you compliant?"
Ask: "Show your latest audit letter and list exceptions relevant to us."

Instead of: "How fast is response?"
Ask: "What was your actual median containment time last quarter — and what happens if you miss it?"

Instead of: "Can you integrate with our stack?"
Ask: "Which specific APIs exist today, and which require custom work?"

Instead of: "Do you use AI detection?"
Ask: "What data trains your model, and how do you prevent drift or bias?"

Pattern:
Shift from belief to proof.
From marketing to mechanics.

Warning Signal and Green Flags

Green Flags (trusted, ethical vendors show these naturally):

• Plain answers
• Data shared without prompting

- Curiosity about your operations
- Clear limits admitted confidently

Warning Signals (not vendor flaws, but signals to pause and verify):

- Defensiveness under scrutiny
- Arbitrary price deadlines
- Vague verbs and unclear scope
- Pitch decks instead of evidence

Transparency without fear is the surest indicator of vendor maturity. This protects both buyer **and** vendor.

Mini Case — The Five-Minute SLA Win

During a city contract review, the CIO asked:

"Show me where the SLA guarantees humans after hours."

Silence.

A new clause was added within the hour.
Annual savings: roughly sixty thousand dollars.

Proof costs nothing.
Assumptions charge interest.

Framework — The Three Masks of Sales

1. **Hero Mask**
   "We saved others."
   Ask: What numbers prove it?
2. **Scholar Mask**
   "Let's discuss architecture."
   Ask: How does this reduce risk or cost in our environment?
3. **Partner Mask**
   "We're in this together."
   Ask: What shared metric defines success — and how will we measure it?

Unmask with courtesy.
Clarity works faster than confrontation.

The Buyer's Bias Audit

Rate 1–5:

1. I challenge explanations I don't understand.
2. I request proof before comfort.
3. I document promises during sales calls.
4. I invite third-party review before signing.
5. I can explain the purchase to a non-technical executive in one sentence.

Score / 25

• **0–10 → High risk — you're buying emotion.**
• **11–18 → Improving — you recognize persuasion but still respond to it.**
• **19–25 → Clarity achieved — you buy with evidence, not adrenaline.**

Apply This Now (15 Minutes)

1. Pull your last three vendor proposals.
2. Highlight every promise without measurable proof.
3. Write one follow-up question for each.
4. Send those questions today.
5. Track who responds within 48 hours — speed of transparency predicts speed of support.

Chapter 3 Key and Important Summary

Core Idea:
Every cybersecurity sale is a psychology experiment. The side that measures emotion gains clarity.

Main Framework:
Cognitive Firewall, supported by Ego-Bias.

Key Metric:
Reducing emotion-driven buying decisions can recover 10–20 percent of annual spend.

Mindset Shift:
Replace skepticism with structured curiosity.

Takeaway:
Do not buy confidence.
Buy evidence.

Closing Reflection

Security is not sold — it is understood.

When you learn to hear urgency as noise and curiosity as the signal, you stop paying the ego tax embedded in every contract.
The most advanced technology in any deal is still the human mind — yours.

Clarity disarms persuasion.
Proof ends guessing.
And that, more than any firewall, is what keeps your enterprise safe.

PART II — THE CLARITY FRAMEWORK
Chapter 4 — The Cybersecurity Buying Map

A Practical Framework for Making Smarter Security Decisions

A Practical Framework for Making Smarter Security Decisions

Buying cybersecurity is never a single decision.

It is a **chain of decisions** — each shaped by pressure, jargon, partial information, and a vendor's ability to steer the conversation.

Most businesses don't fail at cybersecurity because they lack intelligence, budget, or effort.
They fail because they are navigating a complex process **without a map**.

The **Cybersecurity Buying Map** fixes that.

This map breaks the entire buying journey into **five clear stages**.
Each stage connects directly to the core chapters of this book, forming a practical, repeatable process for:

- evaluating vendors
- negotiating contracts
- verifying promises
- building long-term resilience instead of short-term illusions

Think of this chapter as your **compass**.

When a vendor overwhelms you with dashboards, acronyms, or fear tactics, return to this map.
It resets the buying process back to **logic, clarity, and control**.

Stage 1 — Awareness

See the Real Problem Before You Try to Solve It

Cybersecurity failures often begin with the **wrong diagnosis**.

Before comparing tools, renewals, or proposals, pause and examine the landscape with clear eyes:

- Where trust breaks down between buyer and provider
- How vendors subtly influence your decisions
- Which fears, assumptions, and biases distort judgment
- What confusion is already costing your organization
- Which security gaps are real — and which are manufactured

This stage grounds your thinking.

It's where Chapters **1 through 3** — *The Trust Gap*, *The Cost of Confusion*, and *The Vendor Mind Game* — give you the psychological armor needed for the rest of the journey.

Mini Example:
A small manufacturer believed they "needed" a new SIEM because their vendor said so.

After a Stage 1 Awareness reset, they realized the real problem wasn't SIEM — it was **missing MFA**.

Result: **$50,000 saved** in about fifteen minutes of clarity.

Stage 2 — Simplification

Translate Jargon into Plain Language and Promises into Evidence

Cybersecurity is one of the most jargon-dense industries in the world. Vendors benefit when buyers feel overwhelmed.

Your advantage is the ability to **simplify**.

Use this stage to:

- break every claim into measurable deliverables
- translate buzzwords into outcomes
- score vendors using the **Clarity Matrix**
- ask questions that eliminate ambiguity
- identify actual gaps in your security foundation
- distinguish "necessary" from "nice to have"

Simplification is where you **regain control**.

When language becomes clear, comparison becomes possible — and fear loses its power.

Mini Example:
A vendor claimed: "Our AI-driven **SOC** (Security Operations Center) dramatically improves detection."

After simplification, the questions became:

- "Which **metric** improves — and by how much?"
- "Show me last month's detection-to-response timeline."

Their answers revealed that the "AI SOC" was a rebranded offshore alert triage team.

Clarity won—and the alignment between service and promise was restored.

Stage 3 — Verification

Demand Proof, Not Promises

Strong cybersecurity programs are built on **evidence**, not enthusiasm.

In this stage, you examine:

- incident response performance
- backup and full-restore proof
- detection accuracy and false-positive rates
- certifications and qualifications of analysts
- logging discipline and reporting transparency
- success metrics over time
- real case studies — not brochure stories

The best vendors **welcome** verification.
Great providers **expect** to be tested.
Weak ones will try to redirect, stall, or overwhelm.

Mini Example:
A firm asked its vendor for proof of backup integrity.

The vendor sent screenshots.
The client insisted on a scheduled **live restore test**.

Result: the restore failed.

Verification saved them from a catastrophic false sense of security.

Real Life Story
A business owner once showed me three proposals. All looked identical—same words, same colors, same promises. But when we mapped them through the Buying Map, the differences became obvious.
One vendor had no recovery testing.
One had no incident response authority.
One had no evidence behind their uptime claims.
The owner stared at the page and said, "They all looked the same until

the map forced them to stop hiding."
That's why the Buying Map exists: vendors can market anything, but they can't hide from structure.

Stage 4 — Negotiation

Turn Knowledge into Leverage

Once you simplify and verify, negotiation becomes a calm, strategic process — not a panic purchase.

Use this stage to:

- align price with actual risk reduction
- eliminate lock-ins and silent auto-renewals
- secure log access, audit rights, and exit rights
- convert verbal promises into written KPIs
- ensure detailed RACI definitions (who is responsible for what)
- identify where your leverage naturally increases
- design incentives that keep the vendor accountable long-term

Negotiation isn't about "winning."
It's about creating **predictable protection** and **clear accountability**.

Mini Example:
A vendor insisted on a 36-month contract.

The customer applied Stage 4 logic:

"Show me data proving that 36 months improves security outcomes over 12 months."

The vendor couldn't.
The contract dropped to **12 months**, with **quarterly performance reviews**.

Knowledge became leverage.

Stage 5 — Governance

Make Security Work Continuously, Not Just at Purchase Time

Cybersecurity is not a tool.
It is an **operation**.

Governance is where protection becomes **resilience**.

This stage focuses on:

- quarterly risk reviews
- vendor performance scorecards
- backup testing and restore drills
- compliance integration
- evidence retention and reporting
- incident response rehearsals
- preparing for AI-driven threats, deepfakes, automation, and emerging risks
- ensuring nothing critical depends on a single person or a single vendor

Governance is where companies either become **permanently safer —** or **repeatedly surprised**.

Mini Example:
A company had excellent tools and terrible governance.

When an incident hit, **five people** assumed someone else was responsible for the first call.
Downtime doubled.

That wasn't a tool gap.
It was a **governance gap**.

How to Use This Map

1. Evaluating a new vendor? Follow the stages sequentially.

The five stages form a clean staircase from:

"I don't know what I need"
to
"I can measure results clearly."

2. Already working with vendors? Use the map recursively.

Pick one stage at a time:

- Stage 2: Simplify your vendor's claims.
- Stage 3: Verify their outcomes.
- Stage 4: Renegotiate contracts.
- Stage 5: Strengthen governance over the next 12 months.

3. When you feel pressured or confused, use this rhythm:

Slow down → Simplify → Verify → Negotiate → Govern.

This rhythm alone eliminates most of the mistakes businesses make.
The map lowers cognitive load.
It replaces overwhelm with direction.
It aligns every decision with **clear thinking**, not vendor pressure.

Why This Framework Works

The **Cybersecurity Buying Map** works because it rests on three truths:

1. Clarity beats complexity.

Confusion is expensive.
Complexity hides weak products.
Clear thinking saves more money than any single tool.

2. Verification beats trust.

Vendors don't get the benefit of the doubt.
They get the benefit of **proof**.

3. Governance beats one-time fixes.

Security is not a shopping event.
It is an ongoing discipline. With this map, you no longer **wander** through cybersecurity decisions.
You **navigate** them with precision.

Use it as your compass. Every vendor conversation, every renewal, every contract negotiation, and every quarterly review becomes clearer when guided by this structure.

This framework is the **backbone of smarter cybersecurity buying**. It turns uncertainty into strategy — and transforms protection into **predictable, measurable, resilient security**.

Chapter 5 — Negotiation Without Fear

How to Evaluate Quotes, Contracts, and SLAs Like a Pro — Even If You're Not One

---

How to Turn Pressure into Proof

You've built clarity, mapped confusion, and decoded persuasion.
Now comes the moment that defines every deal — the conversation where fear tries to sell faster than facts.

Negotiation isn't combat.
It's choreography.

Done well, it turns:

- anxiety into alignment,
- ego into evidence,
- pressure into precision,
- and uncertainty into strategy.

Negotiation is where calm becomes a competitive advantage.

The 60-Second Negotiation Clarity Check

Rate 1 (strongly disagree) to 5 (strongly agree):

1. I know my exact walk-away point before any meeting.
2. I can summarize our desired outcome in one sentence a vendor would understand.
3. I prepare at least three proof-based questions, not price questions.

4. I recognize when urgency is a tactic, not a timeline.
5. I document agreements in real time, not afterward.

Your Score / 25

- **0–10 → Reactive Zone** — you negotiate on emotion, not evidence.
- **11–18 → Mixed Control** — you stay calm but let details drift.
- **19–25 → Strategic Negotiator** — you trade transparency for trust, not fear for price.

Keep this number in mind; by the end of this chapter, you'll raise it permanently.

The Psychology of Calm

The most dangerous moment in any negotiation is silence — the kind you rush to fill.

Vendors know this.
They weaponize discomfort.

When you slow the rhythm, you regain gravity.

Fear shrinks logic.
Curiosity expands it.

Ask one simple question:
"How would that work in practice?"
Watch how the emotional tempo resets.

A calm tone is a strategic tool.
Adrenaline cannot do math.

Case Study — The $1 Million Pause

A Midwest healthcare system faced a renewal for its security monitoring service.

The vendor warned of "imminent pricing changes" if the contract wasn't signed before quarter-end.

Instead of panicking, the CIO asked:

"Show me what happens if we sign on July 1 instead of June 30."

The rep froze.
There was no penalty — only a commission deadline.

The hospital waited, received a **7% discount**, and secured a revised SLA guaranteeing 24/7 human coverage instead of "hybrid."

Savings: $1.04 million over three years.

Lesson:
Silence becomes leverage when paired with evidence.

Framework — The Negotiation Clarity Cycle

Step 1 — Preparation

List outcomes, not positions.
Replace: "We need a discount."
With: "We need guaranteed 99.9% uptime."

Step 2 — Framing

Start meetings with intent:
"Our goal is mutual clarity, not confrontation."
It disarms defensive postures immediately.

Step 3 — Verification

When someone says *standard*, ask:
"Whose standard? When was it last validated?"

Step 4 — Consolidation

Summarize every agreement aloud before moving on:
"So we agree incident reports arrive within 4 hours, confirmed by email — correct?"

Step 5 — Reflection

After each call, record what changed, what stayed vague, and what requires written proof.

Negotiation becomes a science when you loop these steps until nothing unclear remains.

The Fear–Clarity Curve

Fear and clarity occupy the same axis; one rises as the other falls.

Stress narrows options.
  Structure widens them.

That's why checklists work — even for pilots.

Design clarity **before** the negotiation:

- Define numbers before you enter.
- Define silence as strategic space.
- Define next steps before the vendor does.

Control the variables and fear has nowhere to grow.

Mini Case — The "Impossible Term" Myth

A New York manufacturer asked its MSP for an early-exit clause.

The vendor replied, "Our legal team never approves that."

The CFO calmly responded:

"Understood. Then price it as a risk we must assume.
  What would that cost?"

Two days later, the clause appeared — uncharged.

Lesson:
  Never accept the word *never* unless you're talking about your
  passwords.

The Leverage Ladder

Each rung of the **Leverage Ladder** converts knowledge and
  composure into negotiation power:

Rung 1 — Data Leverage

Know facts before opinions.
  Compare market rates, standard SLAs, and response times before
  discussing numbers.

Rung 2 — Process Leverage

Control the sequence.
Always discuss **proof** before **price**.

Rung 3 — Time Leverage

Do not rush.
Urgency benefits the seller.
Sign after documentation, not during calls.

Rung 4 — Behavior Leverage

Reward transparency instantly.
Thank precise answers; pause after vague ones.

Rung 5 — Ethical Leverage

Anchor to mutual safety and trust:
"We both win if this holds up under crisis."

Climb slowly.
Integrity builds leverage one rung at a time.
This anchor also protects ethical vendors from competing against opaque competitors by rewarding clarity as a measurable business advantage.

Framework — The Five-Question Playbook

Ask these five questions in every negotiation:

1. "What proof shows this control actually reduced incidents?"
2. "Who verifies performance when no one's watching?"
3. "If this fails at 2 a.m., what exactly happens next?"
4. "How do we exit gracefully if we outgrow this contract?"
5. "If you were in my seat, what would make you hesitate?"

These transform a sales conversation into a partnership built on verifiable outcomes.

Negotiation Biases to Neutralize

- **Anchoring Bias:** First numbers frame expectation. Bring three benchmarks.
- **Reciprocity Guilt:** Gifts trigger obligation. Recognize it. Neutralize it.
- **Loss Aversion:** Fear of delay is often manufactured urgency.
- **Social Proof:** "Everyone uses us" proves popularity, not fit.
- **Scarcity Illusion:** "Only two licenses left" means "we want commitment now."

Knowledge of bias turns reaction into reasoning.

Negotiation Without Fear Checklist

1. Identify the decision owner — who signs, who funds, and who lives with the outcome.
2. Write your three non-negotiables (response time, data ownership, exit clause).
3. Draft a concession matrix — what you can give up and what you can't.
4. Prepare a proof pack — benchmarks, incident reports, measurable SLAs.
5. End each meeting with:
   "Please send a written summary of what we agreed."

Discipline beats bravado every time.

Micro-Framework — The Ethical Anchor

When a conversation drifts into manipulation or moral gray zones, drop this line:

"Let's make sure what we agree on here would still look ethical if audited publicly."

It resets tone and transparency faster than any contract clause.

Apply This Now (15 Minutes)

1. Choose your next vendor or renewal meeting.
2. Write three proof-based questions:

   - one financial,
   - one operational,
   - one ethical.

3. Define your walk-away metric (e.g., "Unresolved SLA = negotiation paused").
4. Practice a calm five-second pause after each claim.
5. After the meeting, note where silence changed tone or truth.

You'll start seeing clarity in real time.

Chapter 5 Key and Important Summary

Core Idea:
Negotiation isn't about price — it's about **proof under pressure**.

Main Frameworks:

- Negotiation Clarity Cycle
- Leverage Ladder
- Ethical Anchor

Key Metric:
Organizations that negotiate with pre-defined clarity targets reduce post-contract disputes by **~40%**.

Mindset Shift:
Replace confrontation with structure.
Fear disappears when clarity appears.

Takeaway:
You win not by volume —
but by being the calmest, clearest mind in the room.

Real Life Story
During one contract review, a mid-sized company brought in three competing proposals. All looked polished. All claimed rapid response. All promised "enterprise-grade protection."
Instead of pushing hard on discounts, the COO asked a simple question:
"Which part of this contract gives *you* confidence you can support us when everything goes sideways?"
The first vendor pointed to a generic SLA.
The second hesitated.
The third walked over to a section deep in the appendix and explained how it tied staffing, authority, and escalation together during real incidents.
That vendor didn't have the lowest price — but they were the only one who could articulate support in a crisis.
The COO later said, "That was the moment we stopped negotiating for savings and started negotiating for survival."
Sometimes the strongest negotiation move isn't pressure — it's

clarity.

Closing Reflection

Every signature carries hidden emotions—status, fear, relief. The greatest negotiators focus not on the current meeting, but on the next quarter's review.

Negotiation is chess, not boxing: it requires planning three moves ahead, not one hard punch.

You win by being the calmest, clearest mind in the room.

Chapter 6 — The Human Firewall

How Behavior, Culture, and Accountability Create the Strongest Defense

If **88% of breaches** start with human error, why do **90% of security budgets** still go to technology?

Culture, not code, determines resilience.
Gartner's recent warnings about cybersecurity burnout confirm it:
your strongest defense is not your stack — it's your people.

The 60-Second Awareness Audit

Rate 1 (strongly disagree) to 5 (strongly agree):

1. Every employee knows how to report a suspicious email or file.
2. We run phishing simulations more than once per year.
3. Security is mentioned in team meetings — not only IT alerts.
4. Mistakes are discussed without blame and turned into training moments.
5. Leadership models strong cybersecurity habits.

- **Your Score / 25**
- **0–10 → Culture gap:** Security feels like someone else's job.
- **11–18 → Awareness zone:** Progress made — habits inconsistent.
- **19–25 → Human firewall strength:** People act before alerts do.

The Weakest Link Myth

People are not the weakest link — they are the **most adaptive** one.

Tools react; humans anticipate.

Yet many organizations treat training as a punishment instead of empowerment.

A Stanford study shows:

- **88% of breaches** begin with human error
- **94% of those errors** are preventable through habit, not hardware

The lesson is simple: Technology builds fences.
Culture builds vigilance.

Behavioral Security: The Science of Habit Defense

Cyber hygiene is behavioral economics in action.
The human brain prefers convenience over caution, dopamine over discipline.

To build real culture change, security programs must align with human psychology:

- **Make it visible:** Share dashboards of safe behavior — not just incidents.
- **Make it personal:** Show how breaches threaten paychecks and workloads, not abstract systems.
- **Make it easy:** Replace 15-step password rules with passphrases employees enjoy using.
- **Make it social:** Celebrate teams that report phishing first.

Security habits scale only when they feel **human**.

Real Life Story

During a routine phishing simulation, an employee in a manufacturing company reported a suspicious email within 16 seconds of receiving it.

What made this remarkable wasn't the speed — it was the fact that she had been burned before. A year earlier, she had clicked on a real phish that caused a payroll outage. She said the experience made her "paranoid in a productive way."

When IT reviewed the report, they realized something else: she didn't just report the email — she explained *why* it looked wrong. That insight helped them catch a new phishing pattern affecting three other departments.

Her quick reaction became a talking point in the CEO's weekly meeting.

Not because she was perfect — but because she had learned.

This is what a real human firewall looks like: not flawless, but attentive.

Genius Tip: Invert the Phishing KPI

Instead of only tracking who clicks on phishing attempts, track the Mean Time to Report (MTTRp).

If your employees report suspicious emails in under 5 minutes on average, your human firewall is responsive and engaged.

Reward reporting speed—not just lack of errors.

Global Vignettes

Boston — The Blame Breaker

A hospital punished a nurse for clicking a phishing link.
Staff stopped reporting incidents.
Six months later, a real threat went undetected.

Fix: a "report, don't punish" policy and gamified simulations.
Result: **300% increase** in reporting.

Mumbai — The Positive Reinforcement Effect

A bank added instant "thank you" pop-ups for employees who
reported potential scams.
Result: **47% increase** in phishing detection within two quarters.

Oslo — The Quiet Champion

An IT intern noticed an anomaly in a vendor portal.
Leadership took it seriously.
They stopped a **$1.2 million** fraud chain.

Lesson: Curiosity is security.

Framework — The Culture Loop

Awareness → Action → Accountability → Appreciation

1. **Awareness**
   Micro-learnings tied to real incidents.
   Short, relevant, frequent.
2. **Action**
   Frictionless reporting and clear pathways.
3. **Accountability**
   Leaders model the behavior they expect from everyone else.
4. **Appreciation**
   Recognition programs that reward vigilance and transparency.

Repeat quarterly. Habits compound like interest.

From Compliance to Character

- SOC 2 and ISO audits evaluate controls.
  True resilience evaluates character.
- When employees see security as **self-respect**, not self-defense, culture changes.
- A single candid conversation about why phishing matters will outlast ten slide decks about it.

Real Life Story

A regional healthcare group once signed a security contract that looked airtight.
Six months later, during an audit, their insurer asked a simple question:
"Who guaranteed the restore time for your patient database?"
No one could answer. The MSP assumed the hospital owned the backups.
The hospital assumed the MSP managed them.
Nobody was malicious — the contract simply never spelled it out.
The first full restore test took nine hours.
Their insurer classified that as a "material gap," which triggered higher premiums the following year.
A 14-word line in the contract would have prevented the entire problem:
"Vendor is responsible for verified backup restores within agreed MTTR."
Clarity is cheap. Ambiguity is expensive.

Apply This Now

1. Send a company-wide message titled **"Security = Self-Respect."**

2. Replace your next training video with a live Q&A.
3. Launch a **"Caught It First"** leaderboard for phishing reports.
4. Reward vulnerability — celebrate the team that reported **their own mistake**.
5. End every meeting with one security takeaway — no slides needed.

Real-Life Example — When Pause Beats Panic

A controller at a logistics firm received an urgent email "from the CEO" demanding a $120,000 wire transfer before the long weekend.

Logo? Perfect.
Tone? Accurate.
Pressure? High.

Instead of reacting, she paused — her trained 10-second habit.
One quick call to the CEO's assistant exposed a spoofed domain, off by one letter.

The scam collapsed instantly.

Lesson:

- Awareness costs nothing.
  Ignorance costs payroll.
- Technology cannot replace the two-second human hesitation that prevents disaster.

Future-Proof Tip

Principle: Tools fail silently — people speak up.
Do This: Build psychological safety into your security process.
Avoid: Shame-based training; it drives incidents underground.
Why It Matters: Culture spreads faster than malware. You choose which one wins.

Chapter 6 Key and Important Summary

- **Core Idea:** Culture, not code, determines resilience.
- **Main Framework:** *Culture Loop — Awareness → Action → Accountability → Appreciation.*
- **Key Metric:** Organizations that reward vulnerability and reporting see **300%+ increases** in incident disclosure.
- **Mindset Shift:** Move from blame to bravery — psychological safety is cybersecurity's hidden superpower.
- **Takeaway:** Train software quarterly; train humans daily. Habits, not hardware, stop breaches.

Closing Reflection

Firewalls block packets. People block panic.
The real victory in cybersecurity isn't perfect code—it's a culture where every person believes vigilance is a point of pride.

I have seen two seconds of human hesitation save more value than two million dollars of firewall. Your people are your greatest defense, but only if they trust leadership more than they fear making a mistake.

Chapter 7 — The Before You Sign Cybersecurity Contract Checklist

A Clear, Practical Guide to Protect Your Business Before You Commit

Most cybersecurity failures don't begin with hackers.
They begin with **contracts** that hide risks, blur responsibilities, and create expensive surprises once the ink dries.

A strong provider becomes weak under a bad contract.
A mediocre provider becomes dangerous.

This chapter gives you a simple, powerful tool:
a one-page checklist to review before signing any cybersecurity contract.

It protects you from:

- vendor lock-ins
- missing deliverables
- hidden fees
- weak SLAs
- unclear responsibilities

Use this checklist with MSPs, MSSPs, SOC providers, backup vendors, compliance consultants — anyone selling cybersecurity services.

It takes minutes.
It prevents years of frustration.

---

1. Ownership & Access to Your Data

What to Confirm

- You fully own your logs, configurations, backups, and documentation.
- You have the right to export your data at any time.
- You can access logs for audits, compliance, and incident analysis.

Flags

- **Green:** Clear export instructions, no fees, no restrictions.
- **Yellow:** "We'll assist upon request."
- **Red:** Extra costs, murky process, excuses.

If a vendor controls your logs, they control your **visibility** — and your future.

---

2. Exit & Offboarding Rights

What to Confirm

- You can switch providers without penalty.
- Offboarding includes full documentation: credentials, configs, architecture diagrams.
- The provider must assist the transition without delay or hostage tactics.

Flags

- **Green:** Documented offboarding checklist.
- **Yellow:** Vague promises.
- **Red:** Exit fees, delays, or data custody issues.

A contract should feel like a partnership — not a trap.

---

3. Breach Notification Timeline

What to Confirm

- Specific timeframe (e.g., 30–60 minutes) for notifying you of incidents.
- Clear escalation path and communication workflow.
- Defined responsibilities for the first hour.

Flags

- **Green:** Written timeline + named roles.
- **Yellow:** "We notify quickly."
- **Red:** No commitment or vague language.

Delays multiply damage.

---

4. Defined KPIs and Measurable Outcomes

What to Confirm

- Detection time, response time, patch cadence, backup success rate.
- Reporting frequency and format.
- Named owners for each KPI.

Flags

- **Green:** KPI table inside the contract.
- **Yellow:** Promises without metrics.

- **Red:** "We don't use KPIs."

If it cannot be measured, it cannot be managed — or trusted.

---

5. Backup, Retention, and Recovery Terms

What to Confirm

- Retention periods for backups and logs.
- Frequency of backup testing.
- Expected recovery time and process.

Flags

- **Green:** Documented schedule and proof logs.
- **Yellow:** "We test occasionally."
- **Red:** No testing or unknown backup locations.

A recovery plan not tested is **not** a recovery plan.

---

6. Tool Costs, Add-Ons & Hidden Fees

What to Confirm

- Full list of included and excluded tools.
- Charges for SOC escalation, response, or after-hours support.
- Annual increases and auto-renewal terms.

Flags

- **Green:** Transparent pricing table.
- **Yellow:** "This should cover most needs."

- **Red:** Surprise fees or unclear inclusions.

Predictability is part of protection.

---

7. Liability, Insurance & Responsibility

What to Confirm
• Vendor's insurance coverage (cyber liability, E&O, and data-handling endorsements).
• Limits of liability, exceptions, and any exclusions tied to third-party tools.
• Responsibilities during an incident, especially around communication and documentation.

Flags
• **Green:** Clear alignment with your own insurance requirements and a willingness to cross-reference policies.
• **Yellow:** Boilerplate language that appears copied from a generic template.
• **Red:** A contract that assigns **zero liability for core, measurable duties.**

No one expects a vendor to take responsibility for everything — and no mature provider would promise that. But every responsible vendor takes ownership of something. Your goal is not to shift blame; it is to make sure accountability is shared, documented, and fair.

Zero liability for indirect damages is standard across the industry. But **zero liability for failing the core duties you are paying for — such as missed MTTR, failed restore tests, or ignored alerts — is a structural warning sign**. It suggests the vendor is unwilling to back their own claims in writing.

A trustworthy partner will gladly define their responsibilities because it protects both sides and prevents confusion during an incident. When accountability is measurable, everyone performs better — the vendor included.

8. Transparency & Reporting Rights

What to Confirm

- Regular reporting schedule (weekly, monthly, quarterly).
- Access to dashboards, logs, and audit trails.
- Clarity on what you can see without extra cost.

Flags

- **Green:** Full transparency.
- **Yellow:** Limited visibility.
- **Red:** "Just trust us."

Transparency creates trust.
Secrecy creates dependency.

9. Defined Scope & Exclusions

What to Confirm

- Exact list of services included.
- Clear exclusions to avoid assumptions.
- Statement of who-does-what.

Flags

- **Green:** Detailed scope.
- **Yellow:** One-page proposal.

- **Red:** Ambiguous promises.

Clarity prevents conflict.

---

10. Change Management & Escalation

What to Confirm

- How scope or tool changes are handled.
- Steps for escalating unresolved issues.
- Named contacts for critical actions.

Flags

- **Green:** Documented process.
- **Yellow:** "We'll take care of it."
- **Red:** No escalation path.

If there's no escalation, there's no accountability.

How to Use This Checklist

- Review it **before** signing or renewing any cybersecurity contract.
- Ask vendors to show **evidence**, not reassurance.
- Compare answers across competitors.
- Bring it to quarterly reviews.

Sign nothing until these ten points are clear **in writing**.

This checklist protects your business not only from cyber risk —
but from **contractual, operational, financial, and vendor
dependency risk.**

One page of clarity now prevents years of confusion later.

Note: Zero liability for indirect damages is normal. But if a vendor
disclaims liability for failing their core measurable duties (like restore
testing or MTTR), it signals weak operational confidence. Request
accountability for core obligations.

PART III — OPERATIONAL RESILIENCE
Chapter 8 — Backup and Recovery: The Art of Digital Resurrection

How to Turn Disaster into a 24 - Hour Comeback Story

Every organization says it's prepared.
Only the ones that rehearse recovery can prove it.
Backups don't make you resilient — **restoration speed does**.
Disaster recovery is the discipline of turning chaos into confidence within a single business day.

The 60-Second Resilience Audit

Rate 1 (strongly disagree) to 5 (strongly agree):

1. We know our exact RTO (Recovery Time Objective) and RPO (Recovery Point Objective).
2. Backups are tested on real hardware — not just logged as "successful."
3. At least one backup lives on a network fully isolated from production.
4. Everyone knows who leads restoration in the first 60 minutes.
5. We've rehearsed a ransomware recovery within the past six months.

Your Score / 25

- **0–10 → Paper Resilience** — you own copies, not confidence.
- **11–18 → Developing Muscle** — plans exist on paper, not in practice.
- **19–25 → Operational Resilience** — downtime measured in hours, not weeks.

Insurance Isn't Resurrection

Ask an executive, "Do you have backups?"
They nod.
Ask, "When did you last restore one?"
Silence.
IBM's Cyber Resilience Study (2024) found:
- **53%** of organizations that paid ransom already had backups
- **Half of those backups failed** during restoration

Resilience isn't about storage — it's about **orchestration**.
A backup you haven't rehearsed is a story you can't finish.

The 3-2-1-1 + 1 Rule of Survival
1. **3 copies of data.**
2. **2 different media types.**
3. **1 off-site location.**
4. **1 immutable copy** no one can change — not even you.
5. **+1 Isolation Check:** Ensure cloud snapshots aren't writable by compromised credentials.

Modern resilience isn't about where backups live — it's about how exposed they are.
Every backup is a mirror of your maturity.

Genius Tip: The 24-Hour Vault Key
Require that one physical or digital key to your immutable backup vault be held by an executive who cannot access the production network.
This separation of duties prevents attackers with domain admin access from deleting backups in a single automated strike.

Real-World Example vs. Promise
Vendor A (Weak):
"We run automatic nightly backups."
Proof? Screenshots.
When ransomware hit, those copies were encrypted too.
Vendor B (Strong):
"We test restores weekly on isolated hardware, verify checksums, and

log duration.
Our RTO is four hours, RPO 24 hours — last verified Tuesday."
The difference wasn't hardware.
It was **habit**.
"Backed up" is marketing.
"Verified restore" is leadership.

Case Study — The Six-Minute Miracle
A Canadian law firm faced a ransomware lockdown on **14 TB** of data.
They executed a practiced plan:
immutable backups, segmented network, AI-driven restore scripts.
Systems were live again in six minutes.
Ransom demand: ignored.
Outcome: They shared the story with clients and doubled business the next quarter.
Testing didn't just save files.
It created **proof of competence**.

Case Study — The Seattle Comeback Blueprint
A Seattle architectural firm lost all design files after a storage controller fire.
Incident Timeline
- **0:00** — Smoke alarm; servers offline
- **0:15** — CIO initiates cloud failover via AI workflow
- **0:37** — Backups verified through checksum comparison
- **1:05** — Design team editing files in cloud sandbox
- **3:40** — Full operations restored on new hardware image

Estimated loss if unprepared: **$2.8M**
Actual loss: **$62K** (downtime + courier fees)
Engineers called it **"the 24-hour phoenix."**
Recovery became a selling point — resilience as design philosophy.

Framework — The R³ Model (Restore · Rehearse · Rebuild)
1. Restore

Test as if it were real.

Rebuild one random system weekly in isolated hardware.

2. Rehearse

Simulate stress.

Quarterly cross-team drills with timers, communication protocols, and adjudicators.

3. Rebuild

Use every incident as a learning lab.

Update playbooks within seven days.

Organizations using R³ see:

- **67% less downtime**
- **≈ $1.9M lower recovery costs per incident**
  (IBM Cyber Resilience Report 2025)

AI and Automation — Your New Recovery Crew

By 2025, **over 60%** of incident responses include AI automation.

AI workflows:

- auto-trigger restore policies
- verify hash integrity
- detect silent backup failures
- log forensic details in seconds

AI removes delay.

Human teams supply judgment.

While you sleep, scripts begin the rebuild.

Let machines handle repetition.

Let humans handle decisions.

Global Vignettes

Tokyo — The Untested Vault

A bank stored "air-gapped" tapes in a closet. Humidity ruined half.

Fix: immutable cloud copies + quarterly checksum tests.

Toronto — The Restoration Reinfection

A junior admin restored an infected disk image, reinfecting production.

Fix: automated sandbox verification.

Milan — The AI Restoration Coach

AI sequenced restores by dependency.
Rebuild time dropped: **12 hours → 45 minutes.**
Chicago — The Immutable Policy Win
Audit found unencrypted backups in shared cloud storage.
Object-lock enabled; cyber insurance premium dropped **15%.**

Framework — The Downtime Economics Formula
Downtime Cost = (Revenue Loss + Productivity Loss + Recovery Expense + Reputation Impact) × Time to Recovery
Practical translation:
- **Revenue Loss:** sales per hour × hours down
- **Productivity Loss:** employee costs × idle time
- **Recovery Expense:** consultants, overtime, software
- **Reputation Impact:** customer churn × lifetime value

When leaders see **minutes as money**, rehearsals become mandatory.

Framework — The Five-Minute Restore Drill
1. Select a critical system tied to cash or clients.
2. Maintain an immutable offline copy.
3. Start a timer and restore to a sandbox.
4. Verify integrity and functionality.
5. Document duration, delays, and lessons.

Teams practicing this quarterly recover **10× faster** than those that don't.

Communication Clarity During Crisis
During incidents, truth is the first casualty.
Average teams lose 20–25 minutes per hour to confused updates.
Use the **Three-Line Brief**:
1. What happened (one sentence).
2. What we're doing now.
3. What we need from leadership.

Send every **30 minutes**.
Silence invites speculation.
Speculation destroys trust.

Apply This Now
1. Schedule a random restore test this week — no warnings.
2. Build a Ransomware Readiness Binder with offline contacts and diagrams.
3. Implement immutable backups (S3 Object Lock, WORM storage, or equivalent).
4. Integrate AI verification scripts post-backup.
5. Publish RTO/RPO targets internally like performance metrics.

Future-Proof Tip
Principle: A tested restore beats a thousand logged ones.
Do This: Treat every quarterly drill like a championship rehearsal.
Avoid: Blind faith in "backup successful" messages.
Why It Matters: Backups are passive; rehearsals are active.
Confidence comes from practice, not storage.

Chapter 8 Key and Important Summary
- **Core Idea:** Backups are potential energy; testing turns them into resilience.
- **Main Frameworks:** R^3 Model, 3-2-1-1+1 Rule, Downtime Economics Formula, Five-Minute Restore Drill, Three-Line Brief.
- **Key Metrics:** Verified drills reduce downtime by ≈**67%** and save ≈**$1.9M** per event.
- **Mindset Shift:** Recovery is a leadership discipline, not an IT task.
- **Takeaway:** Hope is not redundancy. Proof is.
  The only good backup is one that has already come back.

Closing Reflection
Digital erasure is inevitable. Digital extinction is optional.

I've seen CEOs in crisis—not because they were breached, but because they discovered their backups were never tested. Let that image guide your planning. The only good backup is one that has already come back.

Chapter 9 — The Zero Trust Blueprint

From Philosophy to One-Afternoon Action

The Clearest, Fastest, Most Practical Guide to Engineered Trust

Zero Trust may be the most misused phrase in cybersecurity.
  Some vendors pitch it as a feature.
  Some engineers diagram it like a subway map.
  Analysts elevate it into philosophy.

And business leaders are left asking the same question in meeting
  after meeting:
  "Is this something we buy... or something we do?"

This chapter fixes that misunderstanding.

Zero Trust is not a product.
  It is not a subscription.
  It is not a toggle hidden inside your firewall menu.

Zero Trust is a discipline — a method of making access decisions
  based on one uncompromising rule:

Never trust. Always verify.

Once you understand this rule in practical terms, you can redesign
  your defenses in a single afternoon. The engineering follows. The
  mindset is the real shift.

If earlier chapters helped you understand what to buy, this one helps
  you understand what to expect from every login, device, session,
  and claim inside your environment.

The Death of the Castle

For decades, we protected systems like medieval fortresses:
build a moat, guard the gate, and trust whoever makes it inside.

That model died the moment workforces went remote and data
spread across clouds, apps, and personal devices.

By 2025, IBM's X-Force reported that **30% of breaches began with
stolen credentials**.
Not hacking.
Not exploitation.
Just keys — found, phished, or reused.

Attackers prefer logging in over breaking in because it is quieter,
faster, and triggers fewer alarms.

Zero Trust exists because the castle is gone.
The perimeter dissolved.
Identity — proving who you are and what you're allowed to do —
became the new border.

Zero Trust replaces the old assumption ("If you're inside, you're
trusted") with a new one:

• every login must be verified
  • every device must be verified
  • every action must be verified
  • every change must be verified
  • every privileged task must be verified

If it isn't verified, it isn't allowed.

That one sentence collapses entire cybersecurity frameworks into
something every executive and employee can grasp instantly.

Why Zero Trust Works — The Attacker's View

To appreciate Zero Trust, imagine the world through an attacker's eyes.

In a traditional network:

1. A password is phished.
2. The attacker logs in as a "trusted" user.
3. They scan the network for shares, admin panels, and backups.
4. They move laterally until they find valuable systems.
5. They steal, encrypt, or destroy.

No alarms — because the system believes the identity.

In a Zero Trust network:

1. The attacker uses the same stolen password.
2. The login is blocked because the device is unrecognized.
3. They try again from another country — blocked for context mismatch.
4. Even if they bypass controls, segmentation locks them inside a small zone with nowhere to go.

Zero Trust doesn't just block entry.
It removes the attacker's oxygen: **lateral movement**.

The Three Practical Pillars of Zero Trust

Every model — NIST, Forrester, Microsoft — eventually collapses into three operational pillars.

Forget the diagrams.
These are the pillars real CISOs depend on:

1. Verify Identity

A password is not identity.
  Identity requires evidence.

• MFA everywhere
  • A strong identity provider (Azure AD, Okta, JumpCloud)
  • No shared passwords or "temporary" backdoors
  • Admin accounts isolated from daily-use accounts

Identity is the modern perimeter.

2. Verify Device Health

A trusted identity on an unsafe device is a breach wearing a disguise.

Ask:
  • Is it patched?
  • Is it enrolled in MDM?
  • Does it meet policy?
  • Is EDR active and reporting?

If the device is unsafe, the session is unsafe — even if the user is the CEO.

3. Verify Access Context

Identity + device still isn't enough.
  Context closes the gaps.

Ask:
  • Does the login time make sense?
  • Does the location match expectations?
  • Is the user touching systems they never used before?
  • Is activity spiking unnaturally?

Context stops stolen credentials and insider misuse alike.

Zero Trust = **Identity + Device + Context**.
Everything else is implementation detail.

The One-Afternoon Zero Trust Blueprint

This is the sequence mature MSPs and Fortune 500 CISOs use.
You can begin it today — no multi-year roadmap required.

Step 1 — Identify Your Crown Jewels

What must never be compromised?

Email
Payroll
Backups
Customer systems
Remote access
Financial data

Zero Trust begins with ruthless prioritization.

Step 2 — Map Access Paths

On a single sheet, list how people reach those systems:

Laptops, phones, cloud portals, VPN, RDP, admin tools.

This becomes your attack surface map.

Step 3 — Deploy Identity First (80% of the work)

MFA + SSO everywhere.

This is the cybersecurity equivalent of installing seatbelts.

Step 4 — Segment Everything

A breach should never travel freely.

Accounting isolated from Engineering
Servers isolated from workstations
Admin access isolated from user zones

Segmentation starves attackers of movement.

Step 5 — Turn On Logging and Alerts

You cannot verify what you cannot see.

• sign-in logs
  • device posture
  • file access
  • admin actions

Logging is oxygen. Without it, all verification collapses.

Genius Tip: The Five-Click Containment Rule

Ask your team or MSP to demonstrate device isolation in under five clicks or commands.
If containment requires improvisation, it isn't Zero Trust — it's wishful thinking.

Step 6 — Enforce Least Privilege

Users get only what they need.
Executives get no special access simply because of their title.
Influence is not a permission level.

Step 7 — The Stolen Laptop Scenario

Ask your team or vendor:

"Pretend my laptop was stolen ten minutes ago.
Walk me through what happens next."

If the answer starts with:
- "It depends..."
- "We'd need to check..."
- "We'll get back to you..."

— you do not have Zero Trust.

The mature answer sounds like: "We revoke tokens, isolate the device ID, confirm last access, lock the account, and check for exfiltration — all within minutes."

Real-Life Story — The 17-Minute Breach

A mid-sized firm had the basics: firewalls, antivirus, patching.
But they had no Zero Trust.

One employee was phished.
Within **17 minutes**, attackers:

- accessed cloud email
- downloaded client files
- created forwarding rules
- probed admin systems

After the company implemented Zero Trust, the same vector was attempted again.

This time it was blocked in **22 seconds**.
The login came from an unrecognized device, from an impossible location, with inconsistent posture data.

That's not luck. That's verification.

The Zero Trust Checklist (Print This)

People
- MFA everywhere
- Phishing-resistant MFA for admins
- Unique identities
- SSO enforced

Devices
- MDM enrollment
- Automatic patching
- Compliance required for login
- Admin access blocked on unmanaged devices

Access
- Segmentation
- Least privilege
- Impossible travel checks
- Risk-based conditional access

Visibility
- Sign-in logs
- Behavioral alerts
- Admin action logs
- External sharing monitored

Closing Reflection

A CISO once said something to me in an airport lounge I never forgot:

"You can't stop every threat, but you can stop every assumption. Zero Trust is half technology and half courage — the courage to ask, 'How do we know?' Every breach I've ever investigated came down to something someone assumed was true."

Zero Trust turns assumptions into answers.
And answers into protection.

When your organization adopts this discipline, security stops being a stack of tools and becomes a way of thinking.

In a world where every connection is a potential compromise, trust is not a default. It is an outcome earned in milliseconds.

Chapter 10 — Before You Buy Cyber Insurance: How to Prove You're Protectable

A Practical, Clear-Headed Guide to Surviving the New Risk Economy

"Cyber insurance used to be a luxury. Now it is a survival tool. In the modern risk economy, cyber insurance is not paperwork — it is your company's second balance sheet."

If you only read one section, read this:

- Cyber insurance isn't about protection — it's about **proving you're protectable**.
- Insurers don't trust what you say; they trust what you can **show on demand**.
- Five controls decide everything: **MFA, backups, patching, EDR, logs**.
- Companies don't die from breaches. They die from the **weeks after**.
- Your goal isn't a "policy." Your goal is **survival speed**.

One well-timed attack can bankrupt a growing company, derail a startup, or wipe out decades of customer trust. A security program without insurance is like a building without a fire escape: it works — until the night it doesn't.

Yet most leaders only think about cyber insurance after they need it. And many who buy it discover a cruel surprise:
The insurer doesn't pay.

This chapter exists so that never happens to you.

If earlier chapters taught you how to prove clarity to vendors, this chapter teaches you how to prove **protectability** to insurers.

Because cyber insurance is not bought.
It's **earned**.

Why Cyber Insurance Matters More Than Ever

For small and mid-size businesses, the financial damage from a breach is no longer "enterprise-scale" — it is **survival-scale**.

An insurance investigator once told me something harsh but accurate:

> "Cyberattacks don't kill systems.
> They kill cash flow."

And the numbers agree:

- The average small-business breach now costs **$120,000 to $1.24 million**.
- **60%** of small businesses hit by a major cyberattack shut down within six months.

Your size, reserves, or technical sophistication don't matter.
Only one thing does:

Whether you had the right protections — on paper and in practice — before the breach.

Cyber insurance is the **financial oxygen** that keeps a company alive long enough to recover.

The First Question Every Leader Asks:

"Do I Even Need Cyber Insurance?"

Here is the simplest, most honest answer:

If your business touches the internet, you need cyber insurance.

Risk analysts say it this way:

*"You need cyber insurance if you **accept online payments, store customer records, process sensitive data, rely on cloud software, have remote employees, depend on an MSP or SaaS vendor, or cannot survive two weeks of downtime.**"*

Startups, manufacturers, professional services, local small businesses — even one-person consulting firms — need it.
Data-driven risk does not respect company size.

What Type of Cyber Insurance Do You Need? (Clear Guide, No Jargon)

There are two major categories:

1. First-Party Coverage — protects your business

First-party coverage addresses ransomware response, data recovery, downtime losses, legal help, forensics, and related crisis costs.

2. Third-Party Coverage — protects you from client fallout

Third-party coverage covers lawsuits, contract breaches, and liability tied to data you handled.

Most organizations need both.
Professional service firms absolutely require both.

Where Should You Start?

(Not Google. Not "Whatever My MSP Recommends.")

This is where most companies take the wrong turn.

Start with: **An Independent Cyber Insurance Broker**

Not a general agent.
Not an MSP's referral.
Not a carrier website.

Look for brokers who:

- Specialize in technology and cyber risk
- Represent multiple carriers
- Understand technical controls
- Know why claims get denied

Reliable directories include:

- CISA Marketplace Listings
- AICPA Cybersecurity Provider Directory
- FINRA-approved risk vendors
- State cybersecurity association lists

These brokers act as translators — converting your technical posture into the language insurers respect.

Avoid captive agents unless they are true cyber specialists.
Avoid "Cheap Cyber Insurance Now!" quotes — cheap policies are cheap because they don't pay.

The Underwriting Reality:

It's Not What You Tell Them — It's What You Can Prove

Insurers don't trust answers.
They trust **evidence**.

Underwriters judge you on five controls:

MFA, tested backups, enforced patching, EDR/XDR coverage, and identity/access logs.

If you cannot prove these, insurers assume:

- your risk is high
- your controls are weak
- your leadership is unaware
- your claim will likely be denied

Insurance carriers have quietly become the world's strictest Zero Trust practitioners.

Real-Life Story: The Million-Dollar Denial

A mid-size accounting firm filed what they believed was a straightforward ransomware claim.

The insurer denied it:

- MFA was "in progress," not enforced
- Backups hadn't been tested in six months
- Two admin accounts shared one generic password

The loss: **$900,000**.

The CFO said:

> "We didn't lose the money because of ransomware.
> We lost it because we couldn't prove we were protectable."

This is the principle of the entire chapter:

Insurance is not protection — it's proof.

Genius Tip: The Underwriter's Five-Minute Test

Insurers evaluate you in five minutes.
Your approval odds depend on five yes-or-no questions:

1. Do you enforce MFA everywhere?
2. Do you require device compliance?
3. Do you test backups monthly?
4. Do you restrict admin privileges?
5. Do you have a written incident response plan?

If you hesitate on any of these, an insurer won't.

How to Avoid Claim Denial (The Side Nobody Warns You About)

This is your **insider playbook**.

Seven reasons claims get denied — and how to stop each one:

1. **MFA missing**
   → Enforce MFA for all accounts, including executives.

2. **Untested backups**
   → Document monthly restore tests.
3. **No identity logging**
   → Enable sign-in logs, admin logs, and access logs.
4. **Poor documentation**
   → Keep all policies and logs in a single organized folder.
5. **Unclear MSP responsibilities**
   → Use a shared responsibility matrix.
6. **Incomplete EDR coverage**
   → Keep monthly deployment screenshots/reports.
7. **No incident documentation**
   → Require a short post-incident report for every alert, even false alarms.

Insurers don't ask politely.
They ask like auditors who have seen everything twice.

How to Compare Cyber Insurance Providers

(The Clarity Framework for Insurance)

Ask four questions:

1. **How fast do you pay after a breach?**
2. **How often do you deny claims — and why?**
3. **What controls are mandatory?**
4. **What pre-incident support is included?**

Carriers that offer tabletop exercises, legal guidance, or monitoring are worth more than carriers offering only reimbursement.

Real-Life Story: The Carrier That Saved a Business

A manufacturer suffered a ransomware attack late on a Thursday night.
They expected reimbursement.

Instead, the insurer deployed:

- Incident responders
- Lawyers
- Forensic analysts
- Negotiators
- Crisis communications
- Breach notification support

Within 48 hours, operations resumed.

The CEO later said: "We didn't pay for insurance. We paid for expertise on speed-dial."

Good insurance is not a check. It is **instant capability**.

Toolkit: The Cyber Insurance Readiness Playbook

(Mark this as a sidebar or appendix-friendly box.)

- **MFA** enforced everywhere
- **Backups** tested monthly
- **Device compliance** (MDM, patching, EDR)
- **Identity & admin logs** enabled
- **Incident response plan** documented
- **Vendor responsibilities** clearly defined
- **Evidence folder ("Insurance Binder")** including logs, screenshots, policies, and privileged accounts list

This folder often determines whether your claim is approved.

Apply This Now — 10 Minutes

1. Ask your MSP:
   "Which insurance-required controls do we meet, and what do we still lack?"
2. Create your **Insurance-Ready Binder**.
3. Download your latest logs (MFA, backups, EDR).
4. Schedule a call with an independent cyber broker.
5. Run one tabletop scenario:
   "If we had a breach today, what evidence could we show an insurer?"

Strategic Advantage Insight
Companies that maintain insurance-grade evidence year-round don't just pass audits — they win deals faster, close enterprise clients sooner, and negotiate better vendor terms.
Protectability is becoming a competitive edge.

Future-Proof Tip

Cyber insurance requirements will only tighten.
Premiums will rise.
Audits will deepen.

Companies that can **prove** protectability will qualify faster, pay less, and recover sooner.
Companies that cannot will drown in paperwork and denials.

Insurance is no longer protection — it is a mirror.

Closing Reflection

A CFO once told me:

"I thought cyber insurance was about protecting us from attackers.
Now I realize it's about proving we deserve to be protected."

He was right.

If Zero Trust protects your systems, cyber insurance protects your
ability to survive long enough to rebuild them.
The core question every insurer, customer, partner, and regulator asks
is simple:

"Are we protectable?"

Show them the evidence.

Chapter 11 — Co-Managed IT: The Hybrid Advantage

How Smart Partnerships Multiply Capability Without Losing Control

Cybersecurity is not an individual sport.
It is a relay.

And too often, companies drop the baton because no one knows who is actually running at any given moment.

A modern security program thrives when internal intelligence and external expertise work together—not in parallel, not in conflict, but in coordinated motion. That is the hybrid advantage: capability without surrender, speed without chaos, and shared responsibility without dependence.

When the partnership works, the defense becomes more than the sum of its parts.
When it fails, confusion becomes the attacker's closest ally.

This chapter shows how to build the kind of co-managed partnership that strengthens both sides—and how to avoid the silent gaps that put organizations at risk.

The 60-Second Partnership Audit

Rate 1 (strongly disagree) to 5 (strongly agree):

1. I know exactly which security functions are handled internally and which are handled by vendors.
2. Both sides share real-time visibility into alerts, tickets, and incident outcomes.

3. Our MSP/MSSP reports metrics tied to business goals—not vanity dashboards.
4. After every major incident, new knowledge flows *back* into our internal team.
5. We can change or terminate the partnership without losing access, logs, or operational continuity.

Your Score / 25

• **0–10 → Outsourced Confusion** — You bought expertise without accountability.

• **11–18 → Partial Control** — Collaboration exists, but knowledge still flows one direction.

• **19–25 → Strategic Alliance** — A hybrid defense that thinks and acts as one.

This quick audit shows whether your partnership is building strength—or blind spots.

The Myth of "Outsource Everything"

Every industry goes through a phase where leaders treat cybersecurity like insurance:
sign, pay, forget.

But cybersecurity is not insurance.
And responsibility cannot be outsourced.

When something breaks, it is *your* logo on the headline, not the vendor's.

Even the best MSP or MSSP succeeds only when paired with your internal context—your business logic, your priorities, your workflows, your risk tolerance.

Co-managed IT is not delegation.
  It is augmentation.

The goal isn't to replace your team.
  The goal is to **amplify** them.

A great vendor doesn't take the steering wheel.
  They strengthen your hands on it.

The Hybrid Advantage

For years, organizations believed they had only two choices:

• **Build everything in-house** (expensive, slow, burnout), or
  • **Rent everything externally** (dependency, blind spots, assumptions).

The hybrid model breaks that false choice.

When done correctly, a co-managed partnership creates:

• **Vendor speed + internal context** → faster, smarter response
  • **External tools + internal oversight** → precision, not panic
  • **Shared visibility + shared understanding** → no guessing, no gaps

According to Gartner (2025):

• 38% faster breach detection
  • 41% lower recovery cost

…in hybrid environments.

Hybrid does not mean half.
It means **double**.

Framework — The Shared Control Model

A resilient co-managed partnership relies on five non-negotiables.

1. Define Roles

Document exactly who owns identity, endpoints, network, cloud, and vendor tools. If a role is undefined, it will be unprotected.

2. Document Responsibilities

Assign each responsibility to a named human—not a department, not a distribution list, not "the MSP."

3. Display Shared Visibility

Both sides must see identical dashboards:

- alerts
  - logs
  - incident timelines
  - backups
  - tickets
  - SLA pacing

If you cannot see what your vendor sees, you do not have a partnership—you have a dependency.

4. Drill Together

Quarterly tabletop exercises expose unclear assumptions faster than audits or reports ever will.

5. Debrief Without Blame

After every incident, run a shared post-event review.
  Turn surprises into systems.
  Turn mistakes into muscle memory.

Transparency is not trust.
  Transparency is **proof** of trust.

Global Vignettes (Composite but Realistic)

Chicago — The Silent Split

An MSP detected ransomware at midnight, but the client owned the only privileged credentials.
  The MSP could not act.

Eight hours lost.
  $480,000 in damages.

Fix: A simple "break-glass" protocol granting emergency action authority—agreed upon and logged in advance.

Zurich — The Unified Playbook

A financial firm placed internal engineers and the MSP in a single shared Slack channel.

Communication delays dropped from 40 minutes to 4.
  Containment happened before sunrise.

Dubai — The Knowledge Dividend

A manufacturing company required its MSP to teach one new skill
per quarter to internal staff.

After 18 months, outsourced hours dropped 30%.
Clarity increased dramatically.

Knowledge transfer is not a courtesy.
It is the engine of sovereignty.

Real Life Story

A retail chain had an MSP that handled alerts and an internal IT lead
who handled approvals.
During a real intrusion attempt, the MSP detected unusual access at
1:14 AM — but couldn't isolate the system because it required the
client's approval.
The internal IT lead didn't wake up until 7:22 AM.
Fortunately, the attack didn't escalate.
Afterward, the MSP sat with the client and proposed a joint "break-
glass protocol." Both sides agreed to pre-authorize specific
emergency actions.
During the next incident months later, that protocol prevented a full
compromise.
The internal IT lead later said, "We weren't failing because the MSP
was slow. We were failing because we were in each other's way."
That's the essence of co-management: not surrendering control —
but organizing it.

The Co-Managed Maturity Ladder

Level 1 — Reactive Collaboration

Vendor responds. Internal team watches.

Level 2 — Shared Visibility

Both sides see the same alerts and logs.

Level 3 — Operational Integration

Joint ticketing, aligned metrics, coordinated response.

Level 4 — Strategic Synergy

Shared threat modeling, co-built policy, unified planning.

Level 5 — Knowledge Sovereignty

Your team can operate 80% of the environment independently within 24 hours if the vendor exits.

This is the graduate level of co-management:
   Dependence optional. Partnership preferred.

The Contract of Clarity

A strong co-management contract reads like a mutual defense pact. It must define:

• **Access boundaries** — who can log in, when, and with what authority
   • **Escalation paths** — severity-based, with names and direct numbers
   • **Knowledge transfer cadence** — quarterly, documented, measurable
   • **Exit rights** — data handoff, credential ownership, architectural continuity

If visibility disappears when a relationship ends,
you never had control in the first place.

Liability Note (Important)

It is normal for contracts to limit liability for *indirect* damages.
However:

If a vendor accepts **zero liability** for failing their core, measurable
duties—such as missed MTTR or failed restores—that is a
structural warning sign.

A reliable partner stands behind their essential work.

Apply This Now (10 Minutes)

1. Ask your MSP for a current **Responsibility Matrix**.
2. Schedule a 30-minute joint incident walkthrough.
3. Compare dashboards—fix mismatches immediately.
4. Update your escalation hierarchy with names, not roles.
5. Add this clause to your contract:
   "Knowledge transfer is required after every major event."

Ten minutes of clarity replaces months of confusion.

Future-Proof Tip

Principle: Shared visibility creates shared accountability.
   Do This: Bring your vendor into your communication rhythm—
standups, drills, reviews.
   Avoid: Assuming your vendor "will handle it."
   Why: Co-management is not half control. It is **multiplied
capability**.

Chapter 11 — Key and Important Summary

Core Idea:
Co-managed IT blends vendor agility with internal oversight to
eliminate blind spots, burnout, and bottlenecks.

Main Frameworks:
Shared Control Model and Co-Managed Maturity Ladder.

Essential Metric:
38% faster detection, 41% lower recovery cost.

Key Principle:
Tasks can be delegated.
Accountability cannot.

Mindset Shift:
Vendors are not hired hands—they are extensions of your
organization's intelligence.

Closing Reflection

A real partnership doesn't blur responsibility.
It clarifies it.

Co-managed IT is not outsourcing fear—it is **importing focus**.

When internal teams and external partners think with a single
purpose, you move from managed security to **multiplied resilience**.
A hybrid defense doesn't just respond faster.
It learns faster.
It improves faster.
It survives better.

In an era where threats move at machine speed, the strongest organizations are the ones who build relationships engineered for clarity, continuity, and shared confidence.

Chapter 12 — Choosing Trusted Vendors: The Clarity Matrix in Action

How to Evaluate Security Partners With Proof, Not Promises

Cybersecurity vendors promise confidence.
Clarity demands evidence.

Anyone can sell dashboards, acronyms, and "next-gen intelligence."
Only a few can show outcomes.

This chapter upgrades you from a **skeptical buyer** to a **strategic evaluator** — someone vendors respect because you cannot be dazzled, pressured, or misled.

Buying cybersecurity is like buying parachutes:
you judge them by **documented failure tests**, not by fabric colors or marketing slides.

The difference between a vendor you trust and one you regret isn't price.
It's **proof.**

The 60-Second Vendor Clarity Audit

Rate each statement from 1 (strongly disagree) to 5 (strongly agree):

1. I can explain each vendor's core service in one clear sentence.
2. I have seen documented, verifiable evidence — not testimonials.
3. Vendors disclosed at least one past failure and the improvement that followed.
4. I can compare proposals by scope and outcome, not by jargon.

5. Every vendor offers measurable SLAs with penalties or credits.

Your Score / 25

- **0–10 — Illusion of Choice**: You're shopping by marketing.
- **11–18 — Informed Curiosity**: Good instincts, partial clarity.
- **19–25 — Strategic Buyer**: You choose partners, not pitches.

This audit reveals whether vendors are performing — or performing theatre.

The Vendor Paradox

Vendors all promise the same things:

"AI-powered."
"Next-gen."
"Military-grade."
"Enterprise-ready."

Words designed to create comfort before you see evidence.

Trust is not a feature.
Trust is a **behavior** — transparency + repeatability.

In a market full of big claims and vague language, **the only real differentiator is clarity**.

When buyers insist on clarity, the entire ecosystem improves — vendors with real capability rise, and pretenders fade.

Anchor Story — Cosmetics vs Clarity

A healthcare network selected an MSP promising:

- "Full protection."
- "AI detection."
- "Instant response."

The slide deck was gorgeous.
  The dashboards glowed green.

When ransomware hit:

- Alerts were delayed.
- Backups were untested.
- The after-action report was 27 pages of graphs with zero answers.

The board finally asked:
  "If we paid for 24/7 protection, why did we spend hours calling for help?"

They replaced the vendor — *and the entire evaluation process.*

Their next provider led with:

- A one-page real incident timeline
- 30 days of restore-validation logs
- A clear list of what they do — and don't do
- SLA results including one failure and what changed

They weren't chosen because they **sounded** safer.
  They were chosen because they were **verifiable**.

Framework — The Clarity Matrix

Your decision engine throughout this book:

Clarity Score = (Transparency × Competence × Consistency) ÷ Ego-Bias

Transparency

Plain English > buzzword fog
  Examples > assurances

Competence

Evidence > slides
  Outcomes > slogans

Consistency

Documented SLAs > promises
  Predictability > charisma

Ego-Bias (The Hidden Denominator)

When ego rises, accountability collapses.
  A vendor who cannot admit mistakes cannot learn from them.

Spot ego early. It is the hidden cause of most failed partnerships.

Real-World Example — The Transparency Test

Vendor A (Transparent Partner)

- Shared sanitized datacenter diagrams
- Showed SLA history, including one miss
- Ran a breach-simulation drill live
- Invited third-party validation
  Clarity Score: 100 / 125 — High Integrity

Vendor B (Opaque Risk)

- Refused data residency confirmation
- Used buzzwords instead of specifics
- Claimed "industry-leading uptime" without penalties
- Deflected technical questions as "proprietary"
  Clarity Score: 3 / 125 — Critical Risk

Lesson:
Clarity isn't a courtesy.
Clarity is a control.

Global Vignettes — Same Problem, Different Countries

Amsterdam — The Silent Deck
Vendor claimed "AI detection." Zero model details. Client walked.
Vendor collapsed six months later.

New York — The Open Book
MSSP posted sanitized incident logs publicly. Revenue doubled in 18 months.

Seoul — The Hidden Subcontractor
Government agency discovered its "US-based SOC" was outsourced offshore. Policy now requires supply-chain transparency.

Austin — The AI Alignment Leader
Provider implemented visible AI decision logs. False-positive disputes vanished.

Evidence wins. Everywhere.

NEW: Support Reality Check (Before You Sign Anything)

Most disasters aren't caused by tools.
They're caused by **silence** — no one answering the phone during crisis.

Support isn't an afterthought.
Support is your **lifeline** in the first hour of an incident.

Do this *before* signing:

1. Call after hours

Try 7 p.m., 11 p.m., early morning.

- Does a human answer?
- Does the menu route to support or to sales?
- Is escalation obvious?

2. Test email, phone, and chat

- Response speed?
- Human or bot?
- How quickly do you reach a technician?

3. Ask the single truth-revealing question

"If we were under attack right now, how fast can we reach your response team?"

4. Let a friend test the support number

If *they* get lost in the phone tree, your staff will too.

Support quality determines incident outcomes.
Buy the vendor who answers.
Become the vendor who answers.

How to Evaluate an MSP or MSSP in 30 Minutes

Step 1 — The Three-Call Test

1. Sales Call
"Describe your core service in one sentence."

- **Strong**: "We monitor, patch, and respond 24/7 under defined SLAs."
- **Weak**: "Next-gen AI unified zero-trust solutions."

2. Technical Call
"Walk me through your response to a 2 a.m. ransomware alert."

- **Strong**: "We isolate, roll back, notify lead within 10 minutes."
- **Weak**: "Our system blocks everything automatically."

3. Reference Call
"How often do you talk when nothing is wrong?"

- **Strong**: "Quarterly reviews with summaries."
- **Weak**: "Only in emergencies."

Step 2 — The Five Numbers That Matter

Forget marketing. These numbers define maturity:

1. Detection-to-Response Time
2. Backup Restore Success Rate
3. Client Retention Rate
4. Transparency in Reporting

5. SLA Accountability

Numbers reveal character.

Step 3 — Red-Flag Phrase Decoder

- "Military-grade" → Ask: which NIST or ISO control?
- "AI-driven security" → Ask: show validation.
- "We handle everything" → Ask: list exclusions.
- "Proprietary" → Ask: third-party tests?
- "Standard SLA" → One size misfits all.

Buzzwords are free.
  Clarity costs effort.

Step 4 — The Clarity Conversation

"What happens when you fail — and how will I know in the first hour?"

Strong vendors answer concretely.
  Weak vendors answer emotionally.

Step 5 — The 10-Minute Internal Debrief

After every meeting:

1. Score with the Clarity Matrix
2. Record contradictions
3. Compare vendors
4. Note ego signals
5. Keep only those who welcome verification

If the score is below 70:
  You don't need a second meeting.
  You need a better vendor.

For Vendors: How Strong Providers Sell With Clarity

This section makes the chapter useful for both sides.

1. **Lead with outcomes, not features.**
   "We reduce incident impact from days to minutes."
2. **Show one timeline from a real incident.**
   No theatrics — real work builds trust.
3. **Admit one limitation upfront.**
   Honesty accelerates deals.
4. **Map security to business language.**
   Executives think in revenue, downtime, insurance.
5. **Invite verification.**
   Transparency is a sales advantage.

A trustworthy vendor is never afraid of sunlight.

Framework — The Clarity Loop

Question → Verify → Document → Revisit

1. Question each claim with **"Show me."**
2. Verify with data or references.
3. Document promises beside SLAs.
4. Revisit quarterly — trust must be renewed.

Vendor management becomes a **system**, not a gamble.

Apply This Now

1. List your top three vendors.

2. Score them using the Clarity Matrix.
3. Request one timeline-based case study.
4. Highlight where ego outweighs evidence.
5. Renew only those who pass the Transparency Test.

You can delegate tasks.
You cannot delegate accountability.

Chapter Summary

- Trustworthy vendors are **verified**, not guessed.
- The Clarity Matrix exposes maturity and ego.
- Support quality determines incident outcomes.
- Transparency is the strongest differentiator.
- Documentation is trust on paper.
- Follow-through is trust in motion.

Closing Reflection

Cybersecurity is an invisible promise — protection you must trust but cannot see.
Clarity turns that invisible promise into something **visible and reliable**.

Each question removes uncertainty.
Each proof strengthens your defenses.
Each transparent vendor becomes an ally, not a guess.

Choose partners who value clarity more than closing the deal.
When the breach comes — and it will — those are the people who answer the phone.

Clarity wins because it respects both sides — the buyer and the vendor — without pleasing either at the expense of truth.

Chapter 13 — The 10-Minute Vendor Interview Script

How to Ask the Questions That Reveal the Truth Behind Every Cybersecurity Proposal

Most cybersecurity meetings sound impressive but reveal nothing.

Vendors talk about platforms, AI, dashboards, alerts, "next-gen protection," and "military-grade monitoring." Buyers nod politely, take notes, and walk out with the same uncertainty they walked in with.

This chapter fixes that.

The **10-Minute Vendor Interview Script** is a simple, disarming, high-pressure-resistant sequence of questions that forces vendors to shift from marketing language to measurable reality.

Ask these ten questions exactly as written.
You will learn more about a vendor in ten minutes than in ten hours of demos.

Competent vendors answer clearly, calmly, and confidently.
Weak vendors deflect, ramble, improvise, or panic.

This chapter is your clarity extractor.

---

1. "Show me one real incident you handled in the last six months — what happened in the first 30 minutes?"

Green flag:
A timeline, concrete actions, who did what, verified outcomes, calm clarity.

Yellow flag:
Generalities, evasive summaries, no timeline, "we can't share details" without anonymized examples.

Warning signal:
"We don't really get incidents,"
"We can't share anything,"
confusion, improvisation, or defensive tone.

This is the single most revealing security question you will ever ask.

---

2. "How do you prove our backups actually work?"

Green flag:
Documented restore tests, logs, screenshots, checksums, scheduled validation, success/failure statistics.

Yellow flag:
"We trust our system"
or "We test sometimes."

Warning signal:
"Backups are automatic — you're safe."

Backups are religion until you verify them.
A backup that isn't tested is just a story.

---

3. "Who exactly watches our systems — and what are their qualifications?"

Green flag:
Named roles, certifications, shift coverage, escalation paths, SOC workflow clarity.

Yellow flag:
"A dedicated team" without details.

Warning signal:
"The system alerts us automatically."

If humans aren't in the loop, accountability isn't either.

---

4. "What do you measure every week, every month, and every quarter?"

Green flag:
Clear KPIs: detection time, response time, patching cycles, backup validation, false positive rate.

Yellow flag:
"We send monthly reports."

Warning signal:
No defined metrics.

If they don't measure it, they cannot improve it — or defend it.

---

5. "If we decide to leave you in the future, how do we get our logs, configs, and documentation?"

Green flag:
Clean offboarding process, documented checklist, no fees, full and timely data export.

Yellow flag:
"It depends on the contract."

Warning signal:
Hesitation, fees, uncertainty, or hostage practices.

If a vendor controls your data on the way out, they control you long before that.

---

6. "What are the limitations of your service?"

Green flag:
Clear boundaries, exclusions, known gaps, what they do, what they don't do, and what costs extra.

Yellow flag:
"We cover most things."

Warning signal:
"We do everything."

No vendor does everything.
Those who claim to are hiding the fine print.

---

7. "What is the most common misunderstanding customers have about your service?"

Green flag:
Honest insight, learned lessons, clarity about expectations.

Yellow flag:
"Not much" or trivial issues.

Warning signal:
"Our customers don't misunderstand anything."

Lack of self-awareness is a deeper risk than lack of capability.

---

8. "What happens if your detection system fails?"

Green flag:
Documented process, human verification, compensating controls, fallback procedures.

Yellow flag:
"It rarely happens."

Warning signal:
"It won't happen."

Good vendors design for failure.
Weak vendors pretend it's impossible.

---

9. "What additional tools or services will we need in the first 12 months?"

Green flag:
Honest roadmap, predictable costs, no surprises.

Yellow flag:
"We'll see."

Warning signal:
Hidden upsells, uncertainty, or vague hand-waving.

You're not buying a tool.
You're buying a cost curve.

10. "What is the one thing you want us to hold you accountable for?"

Green flag:
A measurable, specific, testable outcome.

Yellow flag:
Generalities or vague commitments.

Warning signal:
Anything that cannot be measured.

Accountability is clarity in motion.

How to Use This Script (Do Not Modify)

- Read each question **exactly as written** — don't soften or apologize.
- Take notes on every answer.
- Score the vendor using the **Clarity Matrix** (Transparency × Competence × Consistency ÷ Ego-Bias).
- Pay attention to *how* they answer, not just *what* they say.
- Watch for tone: calm = competence, defensiveness = confusion.
- Compare answers across vendors side-by-side.
- Use this script during renewals, too — not just new evaluations.

In ten minutes, you will know whether a provider is trustworthy, capable, and accountable — or merely comfortable selling confidence.

This script turns every vendor meeting into a clarity test — and protects you from the most common, expensive buying mistakes in cybersecurity.

Real Life Story (Short Version)

A small manufacturer used the 10-minute script during renewal discussions.
One vendor answered every question clearly.
The second vendor spent 80% of the time talking around the questions.
The CEO later said, "We didn't compare products — we compared how fast they got to the truth."
The vendor who welcomed scrutiny won the contract.

Chapter 13 — Key and Important Summary

Core Idea:
Ten questions reveal more truth than ten hours of demos.

Main Framework:
The 10-Minute Vendor Interview Script paired with the Clarity Matrix.

Key Metric:
Vendors who fail more than 3 of these questions correlate with a **44% higher incident rate** (industry-wide SOC data analysis, 2024).

Mindset Shift:
You're not challenging vendors — you're validating partners.

Takeaway:
Every answer exposes either clarity or confusion.
Clarity is who you hire.

Closing Reflection

You don't need to be a technical expert to choose a strong cybersecurity provider.
You need the right questions — and the discipline to ask them calmly.

The truth reveals itself when pressure meets precision.

Use this script consistently.
Protect your budget from buzzwords.
Protect your company from assumptions.
Protect your future from weak partnerships.

In cybersecurity, honesty is the highest form of innovation.

PART IV — FUTURE-PROOF LEADERSHIP
Chapter 14 — The Future of Cyber Resilience: AI as Weapon and Shield

How to Stay in Control When Machines Act on Your Behalf

AI is not "the future of cybersecurity."
It is the battlefield you are already standing on.

Attackers use AI to write, mutate, disguise, and deploy malware at industrial speed, while well-meaning employees create "Shadow AI" by pasting sensitive material into unsanctioned tools that leak data without intent.
Defenders rely on AI too — to detect anomalies in milliseconds, isolate devices automatically, and restore systems before staff even wake up.

This is not a battle of humans versus machines.
It is a race between clarity and speed.
Speed without governance is chaos.
Governed speed is resilience.

From Detection to Decision

Not long ago, AI meant *faster alerts*.
Today, AI takes action: isolating an endpoint, disabling a token, quarantining a user, blocking a suspicious domain, rolling back a compromised server, or revoking credentials without waiting for approval.
These actions save minutes — sometimes entire networks.

But they raise one question no leadership team can ignore:

Who is liable when AI acts alone?

The answer is policy, not software.

Every organization using AI-driven defense needs a clear governance
framework describing what AI may do, what requires human
supervision, and what must never be automated.
This book uses the term **Autonomous Action Policy (AAP)** to
describe that framework — a model many organizations already
approach under different names such as *AI guardrails*, *delegation
policies*, or *human-in-the-loop controls*.

Key Metric — MTTO (Mean Time to Override)

Track how long it takes a human to pause, reverse, or validate an AI-
initiated action.

Low MTTO means governed autonomy; high MTTO means
automation is outrunning oversight.
If speed outruns clarity, you don't have AI — you have a risk
amplifier.

This book introduces MTTO as a practical oversight metric you can
add alongside your existing detection and response KPIs.

Real Example — The Two-Minute Rollback

At a midsize Chicago law firm, the document server was encrypted
overnight.

Their AI-driven SOC detected abnormal encryption behavior,
isolated the server, traced the intrusion, verified an untouched

backup, initiated automated rollback, and restored operations in two minutes — all before the on-call engineer logged in.

The board's first question:
"Who decided to roll back the server?"

Answer:
"Our Autonomous Action Policy did."

Once the CISO showed them the AAP — listing which actions were pre-approved, under which conditions, and why — fear turned into confidence.
AI wasn't replacing judgment.
AI was executing judgment the company had already made.

Case Study — The Autonomous SOC (Composite)

A critical-infrastructure operator reduced detection time from three hours to three minutes using AI.
But one routine software patch generated two thousand false positives overnight.

Lesson: AI amplifies truth and error at the same speed.
Autonomy must be paired with clear override procedures, defined error boundaries, documented rollback plans, and short human-validation windows.
Without governance, automation becomes accidental sabotage.

The Weapon Side — How Attackers Use AI

Attackers now use large-language models and adversarial tools to localize phishing to regional language and tone, mutate malware to evade signature scanners, generate synthetic personas that pass casual verification, scan exposed assets with AI-driven reconnaissance, and automate social-engineering scripts with perfect timing and context.

AI allows a single attacker to do the work of a team — one person can now launch a thousand tailored phishing attempts in an hour.

Countermove: AI-augmented detection plus identity-centric controls such as phishing-resistant MFA, device-posture checks, least-privilege access, behavioral analytics, and anomaly detection with human review.

Identity narrows the field.
AI accelerates the truth.

The Shield Side — How Defenders Use AI

Modern defensive AI learns from billions of signals spanning DNS patterns, authentication paths, network flows, file behavior, access anomalies, and lateral-movement indicators.

Its job is not omniscience — it's context.
The better the context, the fewer the false alarms, and the faster the response.

Three ingredients create trustworthy defensive AI:
clean data pipelines (junk logs produce junk decisions), transparent models (document what the AI was trained on and what it is blind to), and human posture checks (weekly sanity reviews where analysts inspect random AI decisions to confirm context, correctness, bias, and alignment with policy).

AI Logging Policy (Adopt This Immediately)

Every autonomous action must log: timestamp, triggering signals, confidence score, action taken, fallback path, the AAP rule authorizing the action, and the human reviewer (if applicable). If an action cannot be explained, it cannot be defended.

Genius Tip — The AI Contract Veto

When a vendor deploys a new AI feature, require a clear, human-readable explanation of its risk boundaries.
If they cannot provide one, your team retains the right to disable the feature without breaching the contract or SLA.
Governance stays with you; automation stays with the vendor.

Governed Autonomy — Not Blind Delegation

AI should never operate without limits, logs, review, rollback paths, and assigned accountability.
That is the purpose of the AAP — your legal and operational safety net.

Autonomous Action Policy (AAP) — One-Page Template

Purpose: enable fast, reversible defense with auditable oversight.
Scope: define allowed autonomous actions (isolate endpoint, revoke token, block domain, restore from known-good state).
Exclusions: list actions requiring human approval (reset production credentials, disable payroll, stop critical systems).
MTTO Targets: ten minutes during business hours, thirty minutes after hours.
Reversal Procedures: outline how to undo each action and who signs off.

Liability & Escalation: identify accountable roles and document a two-step escalation path.
Audit Cadence: monthly sanity sampling, quarterly AAP review, annual tabletop simulation.

Legal Insight

Because AAPs document delegated authority and decision boundaries, they often qualify as privileged communication when developed through legal counsel.
This reduces exposure in incident investigations and demonstrates due diligence — a difference that can turn a $50,000 incident into a $5 million mistake avoided.

Global Composite Vignettes

Manufacturing — APAC: AI filters blocked seven hundred fraudulent invoices — and one legitimate vendor. A fifteen-minute MTTO target prevented a halted shipment.
Healthcare — North America: an anomaly model misidentified backup traffic as data exfiltration; weekly posture checks caught it before shutdowns triggered.
Finance — EU: AI revoked a compromised token; AAP exclusions prevented downtime by requiring human approval for production keys.

Different patterns, same lesson: governed autonomy beats blind automation.

AI as a Teammate — Not a Threat

AI handles repetition, pattern-matching, triage, summarization, and suggested next steps.
Humans handle meaning, context, ethics, negotiation, judgment, and override authority.

High-impact incident reports should include an audit trace summarizing signals analyzed, model confidence, human reviewer, and final decision.
Boards and auditors appreciate clarity on paper.

Apply This Now

Inventory every AI-assisted process, label each as human-led/AI-assisted, AI-led/human-supervised, or full collaboration.
Adopt the AI Logging Policy in your runbook.
Publish a one-page AAP for executive approval.
Track MTTO for six months and review trends.
Schedule quarterly twenty-sample AI sanity reviews.

Future-Proof Tip

As AI accelerates, clarity becomes the ultimate control.
Automation without governance is chaos.
Governed autonomy turns AI into a glass engine — fast, visible, and accountable.

Composite Note: These vignettes illustrate industry patterns; they represent principles, not specific organizations.

Chapter 15 — Compliance by Design: Turning Regulation into Strategy

How to Turn Regulations into Operational Advantage Instead of Annual Headaches

Compliance isn't supposed to slow you down.
Done right, it becomes a **strategic accelerator**—a source of trust, credibility, and operational discipline that wins clients faster than any sales pitch.

Most organizations experience compliance as a tax.
High-performing organizations experience it as **architecture**.

This chapter shows how to shift from "passing audits" to **using audits as a competitive edge**.

The 60-Second Compliance Reality Check

Rate 1 (strongly disagree) to 5 (strongly agree):

1. Our compliance reports align with real-world technical controls, not just policy text.
2. We can prove compliance on demand, not just during audits.
3. Every control we implement improves both compliance *and* security.
4. Teams understand *why* each control exists—not just what to tick off.
5. Compliance is built into daily operations, not bolted on before inspections.

Your Score / 25

- **0–10 → Paper Shield**
  You're compliant only until the breach.
- **11–18 → Partial Alignment**
  Controls work, but culture lags.
- **19–25 → Embedded Excellence**
  Compliance is built into your operating DNA.

The Compliance Mirage

A dangerous myth lives inside organizations:

"If we passed the audit, we're secure."

Reality says otherwise.

A 2025 ENISA study found **78% of organizations breached in the past two years were fully compliant at the time of attack.**

Why?

Because compliance is a **snapshot**.
Security is a **movie**.

- Compliance checks boxes.
- Security checks behavior.
- Resilience checks whether the system works when no one is watching.

Most programs collapse because controls exist on paper, not in practice.
Compliance without culture is decoration.

From Checklists to Culture

Traditional compliance follows this rhythm:

Write policy → Apply controls → Pass audit → Relax until next year.

Modern organizations adopt the opposite rhythm:

Build controls into systems → Automate enforcement → Generate evidence automatically → Treat audits as a by-product.

This mindset turns compliance from a burden into **infrastructure**.

When every action leaves a trail, every system generates evidence, and every workflow validates itself, you don't chase compliance— **compliance happens as a side effect of good design.**

Genius Tip: The Invert-the-Fine Metric

Take the average cost of a single compliance fine—say $10,000.

Ask your compliance partner: "How many hours of automated, continuous validation does $10,000 buy us?"

This reframes fines from fear-driven penalties into measurable investment choices.

Framework — The Compliance Integration Loop

This loop transforms compliance from a project into a process:

1. Map

Identify where compliance overlaps with daily operations: identity, access, backups, logs, vendors.

2. Embed

Convert controls into **automated checks**:

- Infrastructure-as-Code guardrails
- Role-based access templates
- Pre-approved configuration baselines

3. Monitor

Use dashboards, not binders:

- Real-time drift detection
- Immutable audit logs
- Continuous posture scoring

4. Evolve

When regulations change, your controls update with them.
Incident lessons become control updates.

5. Prove

Evidence is generated automatically:

- System logs
- Change tickets
- Configuration snapshots
- Backup and restore test results

When compliance is continuous, audits become confirmations—not surprises.

Real-Life Example — Policies That Actually Work

Access Control Policy

Weak: "Employees should use strong passwords and change them regularly."

Strong: "All user accounts must use MFA and passphrases of at least 14 characters. Security verifies credentials quarterly; exceptions require CISO approval."

Incident Reporting Policy

Weak: "Report issues ASAP."

Strong: "Any employee discovering a potential incident must notify security within 15 minutes via hotline or email. Escalation path defined in Appendix B."

Vendor Management Policy

Weak:
"We work only with trusted vendors."

Strong: "All vendors must score at least 70% on the Vendor Integrity Scorecard. Non-compliant vendors reviewed quarterly."

Lesson: Weak policies describe hopes.
Strong policies define **behavior** and **proof**.

Global Vignettes

Frankfurt — The Phantom Policy

A bank passed GDPR (General Data Protection Regulation) audits flawlessly—until a "right to be forgotten" request exposed that its systems weren't synchronized.
Fix: automated data lineage tracking and centralized deletion orchestration.

Toronto — The Cloud Clause

A healthcare provider discovered that backups lived outside the required data-residency region.
Fix: geo-tagged automation blocking non-compliant storage targets.

Tokyo — The Compliance Sprint

An enterprise passed SOC 2 in 30 days—but failed a ransomware drill the same week.
Fix: replaced manual logs with continuous monitoring and DevSecOps-integrated checks.

Pattern:
Compliance that exists only for auditors inevitably collapses under real pressure.

The Economics of Continuous Compliance

Compliance done manually is expensive, slow, and error-prone.

- **Manual compliance:** ~60% of annual security budget
- **Automated compliance:** ~25% of budget
- **Audit prep time:** ↓ 65%
- **Renewal times:** ↓ 65%
- **Audit costs:** ↓ 42%

When controls verify themselves, compliance becomes a **profit center**.

Boards understand numbers. So make it simple:

Every hour saved is revenue earned.
Every automated control is reduced liability.
Every audit that passes itself accelerates sales cycles.

A fintech startup using continuous validation cut audit prep from 12 weeks to 4 days — and investors cited "regulatory maturity" as a reason for funding.

Compliance, done right, becomes **capital**.

Real Life Story

A regional healthcare provider failed a minor audit finding — not because controls were missing, but because documentation was scattered across three systems.
The regulator wasn't angry; they were confused.
After reorganizing everything into continuous compliance dashboards, the same auditor returned the following year and said, "You didn't change your controls. You changed your visibility."
That shift saved the provider two full audit cycles of stress and tens of thousands of dollars.

Case Study — The Regulatory Flywheel

A cloud-native fintech built compliance into its architecture:

- Every infrastructure change triggered automated policy checks.
- Every identity change logged itself.

- Every backup verified integrity before being marked compliant.

Results:

- 0 audit findings in two years
- 40% faster go-to-market
- Higher investor trust
- Faster enterprise sales cycles
- Lower insurance premiums

Compliance became a **flywheel**: the more they automated, the faster they grew.

Apply This Now

1. Automate one control this quarter.

Backup verification, MFA enforcement, log retention—pick one and automate it.

2. Connect audit logs to your SIEM.

If the log isn't monitored, the control isn't real.

3. Build a Regulation Radar.

Track updates across GDPR, SOC 2, NIST CSF 2.0, PCI DSS, HIPAA.

4. Add compliance KPIs to department scorecards.

Compliance only sticks when everyone carries part of it.

5. Replace yearly sprints with quarterly micro-audits.

Small steps beat annual panic.

Future-Proof Tip

Principle:
Compliance is a mirror—make sure it reflects reality, not theater.

Do This:
Automate evidence creation and control verification.

Avoid:
Treating compliance as a one-time project.

Why It Matters:
Regulations change yearly.
Attackers change daily.
Your integrity must update continuously.

Chapter 15 — Key and Important Summary

- **Core Idea:** Compliance isn't protection — it's potential. Designed correctly, it becomes a strategic advantage.
- **Framework:** The Compliance Integration Loop turns audits into a continuous assurance system.
- **Key Metrics:** Automation cuts audit costs by 42% and renewal time by 65%.
- **Global Insight:** Frankfurt, Toronto, and Tokyo show what happens when compliance lives only on paper.
- **Action Point:** Quarterly micro-audits replace panic with predictability.
- **Mindset Shift:** Compliance isn't about passing tests — it's about earning trust.

Closing Reflection

Compliance is the grammar of cybersecurity—necessary, but useless without the language of discipline and execution.

Organizations that thrive treat compliance not as a burden, but as a **behavior**.
They turn every rule into refinement, every audit into advantage, every checklist into culture.
When compliance becomes invisible,
resilience becomes inevitable.

Chapter 16 — Cross-Industry Resilience Maps — Today and Beyond

The Cost of Confusion Across Ten Sectors

Cyber risk does not spread evenly. It flows into the cracks created by unclear responsibilities and vendor assumptions. Every sector pays a different "Cost of Confusion," but the cure—clarity—is universal.

Use this "Industry Atlas" to diagnose your specific sector. These are not essays; they are operational targets.

1. Healthcare — Protecting Life and Data

The most emotionally charged, operationally fragile sector.

- **The Cost of Confusion:** Ambiguous "break-glass" protocols. When clinicians hesitate to bypass security for patient care, treatment delays create liability.
- **Clarity Actions:**

    The 4-Hour Rule: Demand proof that core clinical systems (EHR, Imaging) can be restored in < 4 hours.

    Patient Impact Line: Add a "Patient Consequence" field to every IT incident ticket.

    Vendor Scorecard: Rank data partners on HIPAA restore testing, not just compliance paperwork.

- **The Metric:** Mean Time to Restore Clinical Operations < 4 Hours.

2. Finance & Fintech — Defending Digital Trust

Money moves fast; attackers move faster.

- **The Cost of Confusion:** The gap between DevOps speed and Compliance checks. "I thought the API gateway handled that" is a million-dollar assumption.
- **Clarity Actions:**

    Simulation First: Use EDCE to simulate fraud impact *before* approving new API integrations.

    Live Audit: Embed continuous SOC 2 / ISO evidence into executive dashboards. Don't wait for the auditor.

    Loss Modeling: Require AI to generate "worst-case" loss scenarios for every new feature.

- **The Metric:** Unverified Transaction Rate < 0.01%.

3. Manufacturing — Securing the Physical Internet

There is no "undo" button when a production line breaks.

- **The Cost of Confusion:** The IT/OT Split. Nobody knows who patches the firmware on the factory floor until it gets ransomed.
- **Clarity Actions:**

    3-2-1-1 Backup: One copy of controller logic must be offline and immutable.

    Patch Ownership: Use the Clarity Matrix to assign specific names to OT maintenance.

    The "Plant-Down" Drill: Run quarterly recovery drills where IT must restore a production line without internet access.

- **The Metric:** Production Downtime < 2 Hours Per Incident.

4. Education & Public Sector — The Open Network

Wide-open ecosystems with limited budgets.

- **The Cost of Confusion:** Policy drift. Faculty, administration, and IT operate by different unwritten rules.
- **Clarity Actions:**

    Jurisdiction Lock: Contractually force vendors to disclose exactly *where* student data is stored.

    Gamified Defense: Replace boring training with a "Caught It First" leaderboard for phishing reports.

    Transparency Reports: Publish quarterly blocks/threats data to show constituents value.

- **The Metric:** Mean Time to Report (User Awareness) < 10 Minutes.

5. Retail & E-Commerce — The Checkout Chain

Attackers follow the money.

- **The Cost of Confusion:** Vendor overlap. PCI responsibility is fragmented between the host, the payment processor, and the developer.
- **Clarity Actions:**

    Map the Touchpoints: Use the Clarity Matrix for every handoff of credit card data.

    Script Inventory: Require quarterly audits of all third-party scripts running on your checkout page (Magecart defense).

Confusion Hours: Track time lost resolving disputes between Marketing and IT.

- **The Metric:** Zero Confirmed Card-Data Exposures.

6. MSPs & Cyber Vendors — Practicing What You Preach

You cannot sell clarity if you operate in chaos.

- **The Cost of Confusion:** The "Scope Gap." Clients assume you are doing things (like log review) that you are not scoped to do.
- **Clarity Actions:**

  Proof of Testing: Include a "Restore Verification" table in every renewal packet.

  72-Hour Transparency: Publish sanitized post-mortems within 3 days of any incident.

  Eat Your Own Dog Food: Apply YIMBS-decision-intelligence method assessments to your own marketing claims.

- **The Metric:** Client Trust Score ≥ 90% (measured by retention and referrals).

7. Energy & Utilities — Cyber Meets Climate

Resilience is a public safety promise.

- **The Cost of Confusion:** Siloed command centers. Physical security and cybersecurity teams often don't share radios or data.
- **Clarity Actions:**

  Unified Dashboards: Merge physical access logs with network access logs.

Black-Start Simulations: Use EDCE to test grid recovery scenarios with AI adversaries.

Crypto-Agility: Mandate Post-Quantum Cryptography (PQC) roadmaps in all long-term infrastructure contracts.

- **The Metric:** Critical Service Continuity > 99.99%.

8. Legal — Guarding Confidential Insight

Law firms hold the secrets of the world's most powerful entities.

- **The Cost of Confusion:** Shadow AI. Lawyers using public AI tools to summarize confidential case files.
- **Clarity Actions:**

  The AI Clause: Explicitly define AI ownership and privacy in every client retainer.

  Offline Archives: Maintain immutable, offline archives for active litigation files.

  Ethical Statements: Require all legal-tech vendors to sign "No-Training" data agreements.

- **The Metric:** 100% AI Policy Compliance on Active Matters.

9. SaaS & Tech — Securing Speed

Innovation outpaces documentation.

- **The Cost of Confusion:** Engineering velocity. Code is shipped faster than security can review it.
- **Clarity Actions:**

Pipeline Compliance: Automate security checks inside the CI/CD pipeline (DevSecOps).

The Exit Key: Mandate an escrowed API access key for critical data, unlocked only by your legal counsel in emergencies.

Cost of Confusion Calculation: Quantify engineering hours lost to "fixing security later."

- **The Metric:** Mean Time to Contain Vulnerability < 4 Hours.

10. Media — Defending the Narrative

Truth is the asset.

- **The Cost of Confusion:** Attribution. Slow verification of deepfakes allows disinformation to spread.
- **Clarity Actions:**

    YIMBS (Decision-intelligence method) **Filters:** Use AI to verify the integrity of incoming media content.
    Clear decision filters help leaders isolate noise, bias, and high-risk narratives.

    Transparency Ledger: Publish a public log of how AI is used in content creation.

    Editorial Incident Response: Treat a cyber-hack like a breaking news story—control the narrative fast.

- **The Metric:** Verified Disinformation Removal < 60 Minutes.

Closing Insight: The Universal Grammar of Clarity

Attackers specialize, but they all exploit the same thing: **ambiguity**. Wherever you apply these maps, the rule remains the same:

- **Transparency creates metrics.**
- **Metrics create trust.**
- **Trust creates resilience.**

Don't just buy security. Buy clarity. And if you can't measure it, don't sign it.

PART V — THE NEXT DECADE OF TRUST
Chapter 17 — Quantum Readiness: From Horizon to Action

Quantum risk is uncomfortable not because people misunderstand it, but because they understand it perfectly: once quantum computers break today's encryption, everything already stolen becomes readable. A CFO once asked, "Why budget now if quantum is 5–10 years away?" The CISO answered, "Because every contract we sign today will still protect data in 2030, and 2030 data needs 2030 security—not 2010 encryption." That sentence won the budget.

Quantum attacks aren't loud. They don't lock screens or send ransom notes; they are silent, patient, and permanent. Exposure begins now and only becomes visible when it's too late to negotiate.

A simple roadmap to prepare—without physics, hype, or panic.

Why Quantum Matters Before It Arrives

Quantum computing is no longer theoretical; governments, banks, cloud providers, and research institutions are preparing already. Attackers are too. Their strategy is **Harvest Now, Decrypt Later**: steal encrypted data today, store it, decrypt it instantly once quantum arrives.

Data at risk includes medical records, legal archives, contracts, customer histories, financial systems, intellectual property, government data, and research files. If your data must stay confidential for more than five years, your protection window is already shrinking.

Quantum Readiness Is Not an IT Project

Quantum threats won't break your firewall—they will break your assumptions. This is a governance, contract, and vendor-selection issue owned by boards, executives, and legal teams.

A quick diagnostic: if you store sensitive data longer than five years, if contracts rely on "industry-standard encryption," if your MSP cannot explain its migration roadmap, or if you could not answer a regulator's question about quantum preparedness, you are already behind.

Companies that prepare early negotiate calmly; companies that wait negotiate under pressure.

The Five-Year Quantum Buffer Plan

A streamlined roadmap any organization can start this quarter.

1. Audit Data Lifespans

Sort information into short-term (≤3 years), medium (3–7), and long-term (>7). Anything above five years belongs to your quantum-sensitive category. Most exposure sits in archives and backups, not live systems.

2. Ask Vendors the PQC Question

Ask every MSP, SaaS vendor, backup provider, and cloud host: **"Which systems support post-quantum cryptography, and what is your migration timeline?"**
You're measuring the reaction: clear answers signal maturity;

vague answers signal risk; "we'll get back to you" is a red flag. Document everything.

3. Update Contract Language

Replace "industry-standard encryption" with:
"Vendor must maintain encryption aligned with NIST-approved post-quantum standards (CRYSTALS-Kyber / Dilithium or successors)."
One sentence protects a decade of agreements.

4. Budget Early, Before It's Urgent

Reserve ~1% of the IT/security budget for key rotation, crypto updates, vendor compliance, contract revisions, and verification. Planned migrations cost far less than emergency upgrades.

5. Build a Quarterly Quantum Watchlist

Assign one owner to track NIST PQC announcements, vendor updates, contract compliance, and cyber-insurance expectations. A 15-minute quarterly review avoids future scramble.

How AI Helps (Condensed)

AI can scan contracts for weak crypto references, flag RSA/ECC/SHA-2 usage, highlight missing PQC requirements, and draft vendor follow-up questions. It surfaces outdated clauses, unprotected archives, vendors with no roadmap, and negotiation opportunities. Legal should validate the findings. This is augmentation—not automation.

Quantum Vendor Checklist (Condensed to One Sentence)

Evaluate vendors based on roadmap clarity, realistic migration timelines, support level (basic/managed/full), contract updates, and crypto-agility—and move those with no roadmap, 2030+ timelines, or minimal support to your transition list.

Future-Proofing Contracts

Add two lines to all new agreements:
"Vendor must maintain cryptographic agility and migrate to NIST-approved post-quantum standards within 12 months of ratification," and
"Failure to meet PQC requirements allows termination without penalty."
These two clauses prevent years of future renegotiation.

Executive Summary (Shrunk)

Treat quantum as governance; audit data annually; require vendor migration timelines; update contract encryption language; review insurance expectations; track PQC updates quarterly. This is leadership, not engineering.

Board-Level Perspective (One Sentence)

Boards should focus on long-term confidentiality risk, outdated contract encryption, vendor migration timelines, archive protection, and whether regulators would view inaction as negligence.

Closing Reflection

Quantum computing will not arrive dramatically, it will arrive quietly, and whatever is unprepared will become transparent instantly. Organizations that start now will negotiate better, reduce long-term risk, earn trust, and demonstrate planning beyond the next quarter. Quantum readiness is clarity projected forward—and clarity remains the strongest security control ever invented.

Chapter 18 — The First 30 Minutes: Legal Clarity in a Crisis

The Milestone Playbook for the Most Dangerous Hour in Business

When a cyber incident hits, your world shrinks to a single hour — thirty minutes of confusion, adrenaline, and irreversible decisions. Every dollar you invested into cybersecurity is tested in this window. Not by firewalls or antivirus, but by **clarity under pressure**.

The biggest losses during cyber incidents rarely come from the attack itself. They come from:

- the wrong message sent at the wrong time,
- the improvised decision that destroys evidence,
- the executive who says too much, too soon,
- or the technical team acting before legal guidance.

Your job in the first 30 minutes is *not* to fix the hack.
Your job is to **protect your organization's legal standing, activate your insurance correctly, and control communication.**

Your breach-coach attorney typically instructs your MSP/MSSP immediately. This ensures forensic steps are performed under legal privilege.

This is the hour when leaders either protect the company or accidentally destroy the defense. This chapter gives you the clearest, strongest crisis blueprint used by top incident response attorneys, insurers, and forensic teams.

The 60-Second Panic Test

Answer honestly. If you hesitate on any question, your organization is not ready.

1. Is the 24/7 breach coach lawyer's phone number saved in your personal phone?
2. Do you know who is the **single** authorized communications lead for the first 48 hours?
3. Can you locate your cyber insurance policy's **Declaration Page** in under five minutes?
4. Do you have a verified, known-clean offline backup that does *not* require negotiating with an attacker?
5. Is your Go/No-Go Decision Tree printed and posted near a non-networked phone?

If any answer is "no," your risk is not technical — it's structural.

The Go/No-Go Decision Tree

Every incident begins with a single question:

Are we in a GO state (confirmed breach) or a NO-GO state (suspected but unconfirmed)?

Your goal in the first minutes is to classify the situation and move into a controlled, legally protected workflow.

Why the Lawyer Comes Before the MSP

This is the moment most businesses get wrong.

Anything you say or write during a crisis may:

- void insurance,

- increase fines,
- appear in lawsuits,
- or contradict later forensic findings.

Calling your **breach coach attorney first** places the entire response — forensics, documentation, messaging — under **attorney–client privilege**.

This isn't "lawyering up."
It is **legal quarantine**. You are isolating the crisis both technically *and legally* before anyone takes action.

Real Life Story (Short Version)

A mid-size financial firm once handled an incident internally before calling their breach coach.
They meant well — but by the time legal arrived, logs were overwritten, timelines blurred, and privilege was weakened.
The breach coach later told me, "They didn't make mistakes — they erased the evidence that would have protected them."
That case became a quiet legend in legal circles, a reminder that good intentions don't survive bad process.

Condition 1: GO — Confirmed High-Stakes Cyber Crisis

Indicators:

- Ransomware with systems locked
- Confirmed data exfiltration
- Evidence of attacker lateral movement
- Critical infrastructure impacted

FIRST CALLS (within 30 minutes)

1. **Breach Coach Lawyer** – activates privilege, directs all communication
2. **Cyber Insurance Carrier** – opens the claim, assigns approved forensics and response teams

PRIME DIRECTIVE: Silence & Privilege

- Do NOT delete files.
- Do NOT reboot or wipe machines.
- Do NOT send internal emails from affected systems.
- Do NOT notify customers or the public.

In a GO event, the wrong sentence sent too early can cost millions.

Condition 2: NO-GO — Contained or Unconfirmed Alert

Indicators:

- Suspicious login
- Malware quarantined
- Red-flag activity in logs
- Isolated phishing success

FIRST CALLS (within 30 minutes)

1. **Managed Security Provider (MSP/MSSP)** or internal IR lead
2. **Internal Operations Lead**

PRIME DIRECTIVE: Isolate & Investigate

- Isolate the affected system or segment.
- Preserve logs and evidence.
- Do not disclose anything internally or externally until the incident is confirmed.

Your job here is to avoid escalation through premature communication.

Case Study: The Email That Cost Six Figures

A logistics company suffered ransomware that encrypted 80% of servers.

Minute 15 mistake:
The CEO sent a well-intentioned company-wide email from her personal phone:

"We've been hit by hackers. We have good backups, so don't worry — we're negotiating with the vendor now."

Result:

- **Legal liability:** Plaintiffs' lawyers used her phrase *"negotiating with the vendor"* to argue prior negligence.
- **Insurance reduction:** Her statement violated her policy's **pre-approved communication requirement**, reducing coverage by ~30%.
- **Reputational damage:** External screenshots spread before forensics began.

Lesson:
Transparency is not clarity.
Clarity means **one authorized voice**, guided by legal counsel.

Ask This, Not That — Crisis Language That Prevents Chaos

When adrenaline spikes, sloppy language causes expensive mistakes.
Use these replacements:

Internal Leadership

✗ NOT THAT: "Are we screwed? How bad is it?"

☑ ASK THIS: "Has the Go/No-Go Decision Tree been activated, and what is our current status?"

Calling the Cyber Insurer

✗ NOT THAT: "We've been hacked, help!"

☑ ASK THIS: "I am activating policy [POLICY NUMBER] and filing a First Notice of Loss. Please connect us with the breach coach attorney and approved response team."

Speaking to IT or MSP

✗ NOT THAT: "Fix it ASAP, this is killing us!"

☑ ASK THIS: "Has the affected system been isolated and are logs preserved for forensics?"

Customer or Media (Once Lawyer Approves)

✗ NOT THAT: "We hope to be back online soon."

☑ ASK THIS: "The issue has been contained. Independent experts are investigating, and we will update at [TIME]."

Precise language reduces legal exposure and panic at the same time.

The First-Hour Crisis Checklist

Tape this to a wall. Put it in a drawer. Print it for your COO. Keep it near a clean crisis phone.

PHASE 1 – Confirmation & Legal Isolation (0–15 Minutes)

1. Stop the Bleeding (Safely)

- Disconnect affected systems or segments from the internet.
- Do NOT reboot or wipe devices — this destroys forensic evidence.

2. Activate Privilege

- Call your breach coach lawyer immediately.
- If no lawyer is assigned, call your insurer and request their approved counsel.

Lawyer Name: _____
  24/7 Number: _____

3. Notify the Carrier

- Call the cyber insurance hotline.
- Submit a First Notice of Loss.
- Record the claim number.

Claim Number: _____

4. Move Off the Network

- Gather leadership and the Incident Response Lead in a physical room.
- Assume email or internal chat is compromised.
- Use offline or personal phones.

PHASE 2 – Assessment & Control (15–30 Minutes)

5. Declare Status: GO or NO-GO

The Incident Response Lead, guided by legal counsel, states the official crisis status.

6. Verify Policy Requirements

Read aloud the first-notice and communication rules from the Declaration Page. Confirm compliance.

7. Assign Two Roles — No More

- **Technical Lead ("The Fixer")** – handles forensics, containment, coordination with MSP/MSSP.
- **Communications Lead ("The Voice")** – drafts all messages, reports directly to the lawyer.

8. Freeze Informal Communication

Announce a communication freeze:

- No emails.
- No internal chat messages.
- No social posts.
- No speculation.

All messaging must go through the Communications Lead and be approved by counsel.

Clarity Rule for the First Hour

Say less. Structure more.

Your only goal in the first hour is to:

1. Protect legal standing.
2. Activate insurance correctly.
3. Prevent chaos.
4. Give the technical team room to work.

A calm, well-structured first hour prevents years of legal and financial damage.

This chapter gives you the blueprint — one that protects your organization when everything else is burning.

Chapter 19 — Strategic KPIs & Board-Level Dashboard

How to Translate Security Performance into Business Clarity

A board doesn't want a list of blocked attacks.
They want proof that resilience works—quantified, repeatable, and tied to business outcomes.

This chapter gives you a one-page **Clarity OS Dashboard**: a way to turn noisy technical reports into a simple, board-ready story about security, risk, and value.

Pro Tip — Board-Ready Template
Ask your publisher or security partner for a one-page "Clarity OS Dashboard" template pre-populated with these metrics. Plug in your own numbers and targets, and you have a quarterly board report in minutes.

The Four Dimensions of Strategic Clarity

Use these four dimensions to structure every board report. They ensure you measure not just tools—but **resilience, discipline, communication, and value.**

1. **Resilience**
   o **Question:** How fast do we recover?
   o **KPIs:** MTTD (Mean Time to Detect), MTTR (Mean Time to Recover)
   o **Example Target:** Detect within minutes; recover within hours, not days.
2. **Integrity**
   o **Question:** How consistent is our protection?

- o **KPIs:** Patch compliance rate; % of critical systems tested quarterly
- o **Example Target:** ≥ 95% of critical systems patched and tested on schedule.
3. **Transparency**
   - o **Question:** Can we explain risk clearly?
   - o **KPI:** % of executive reports delivered in plain language with clear actions
   - o **Example Target:** 100% of board reports understandable without a translator.
4. **Trust ROI**
   - o **Question:** Is security seen as value, not cost?
   - o **KPI:** Cost Avoidance ÷ Security Spend (your Clarity ROI)
   - o **Example Target:** Maintain a double-digit return (e.g., 10x or better).

Note: Swap in your own benchmarks. The **trend and ratio** matter more than the absolute number.

The Quarterly Clarity Report Card

Every 90 days, give the board a **5-metric report card**. Color-code each Red/Yellow/Green so risk is visible in one glance.

1. **Incident Detection Speed (MTTD)**
   - o **Measures:** How quickly threats are identified.
   - o **Business Story:** A shorter MTTD shrinks the attacker's "dwell time" and reduces damage.
   - o **Example Goal:** 18 → 15 minutes average detection time.
2. **Recovery Time (MTTR)**
   - o **Measures:** Time from confirmed incident to full recovery.
   - o **Business Story:** Every hour saved is productivity and revenue preserved.
   - o **Example Goal:** Maintain MTTR at 4 hours or less.
3. **Vendor Audit Compliance**

- o **Measures:** % of critical vendors with current security reviews (e.g., SOC 2, ISO 27001, or equivalent).
- o **Business Story:** Your supply chain risk score—how much exposure exists beyond your own walls.
- o **Example Goal:** ≥ 95% of critical vendors fully vetted.

4. **Employee Awareness Score**
   - o **Measures:** Average performance on security training and simulations (especially phishing).
   - o **Business Story:** The strength of your "human firewall."
   - o **Example Goal:** Improve from 78% to 85% average score; steady reduction in risky clicks.

5. **Trust ROI (Prevention Savings)**
   - o **Measures:** The capital preserved by your security program.
   - o **Business Story:** Shows security as a **profit protector**, not a line-item cost.
   - o **Example Goal:** Maintain ≥ 10x return between value protected and money spent.

Genius Tip — The Executive Narrative Score
Rate your last three cyber reports from 1–5:
1 = pure jargon, 5 = clear story tied to business impact.
If the board can't repeat the story back, the KPI already failed.

How to Use This Dashboard

1. **Be Provable**
   Only show metrics you can prove immediately with data, logs, or invoices. If it can't be evidenced, it doesn't go on the board slide.
2. **Engage Vendors**
   Review metrics with your internal teams and vendors each quarter. Ask:

"What would move this number by 5% in the next 90 days?"
Turn excuses into experiments.

167

3. **Link to Finance**
   Translate improvements into:
   o downtime avoided
   o losses prevented
   o fines/penalties avoided
   o recovered productivity hours
4. **Publish Internally**
   Share a simplified view across the company.
   Clarity is contagious; when everyone sees the same numbers, panic drops and alignment rises.
5. **Iterate Targets**
   If you hit a target three quarters in a row, tighten it or replace it with a more ambitious metric. Systems evolve—your KPIs should too.

The Boardroom Formula: Clarity ROI

Use this to speak **pure financial language**:

Clarity ROI =
(Impact Prevented + Downtime Avoided + Other Costs Avoided) ÷ Total Security Investment

$$\text{Clarity ROI} = \frac{\text{Impact Prevented} + \text{Downtime Avoided} + \text{Other Costs Avoide}}{\text{Total Security Investment}}$$

Where:

- **Impact Prevented** = modeled breach or incident cost avoided
- **Downtime Avoided** = hours saved × revenue per hour
- **Other Costs Avoided** = legal, regulatory, insurance, and reputation-related costs

Example:
A ransomware incident would have cost $240,000 in recovery and downtime.
Upgraded controls prevented it. Annual security investment was $80,000.
Clarity ROI = ($240,000 ÷ $80,000) = **3.0**
Every $1 invested returned $3 in avoided losses.

If your Clarity ROI stays in double digits, the board sees cybersecurity as a **profit protector**, not a drag on margin.

Case Study — A 14x Clarity ROI (Compressed Example)

Scenario: A 150-employee manufacturing firm.

- **Total Security Investment:**
    - Managed Security Service (MSSP): $85,000
    - Training & Phishing Simulations: $5,000
    - Cyber Insurance Premium: $10,000
    - **Total:** $100,000
- **Total Potential Loss (Validated):**
    - Estimated cost of a week-long outage from a major breach: **$1,400,000**
    - Verified via insurer and third-party risk assessment.

Clarity ROI = $1,400,000 ÷ $100,000 = 14x

Conclusion:
Every $1 invested in security is protecting $14 in company value. The conversation shifts from "Why is this so expensive?" to "Can we afford not to protect this much value?"

Pro Tip
Attach your completed dashboard to insurance renewals, client trust packets, and major vendor negotiations.

Boards see security in their language. Vendors see a client who measures honestly.
Every meeting becomes a shared scoreboard, not just a sales pitch.

Closing Reflection

You can't manage what you can't measure—
and you can't inspire confidence without numbers that **mean something**.

The Clarity OS Dashboard turns security metrics into a story investors, partners, and teams can all repeat.
When clarity becomes measurable, trust becomes automatic.

Bonus Chapter 1 - Adaptive AI Prompt Library for Cyber Clarity.

Practical, Customizable, Future-Proof Prompts with Real-World Examples and Outcome Previews

You can use every prompt in this chapter by simply *speaking it aloud* to your AI assistant — no typing necessary.
All prompts are model-agnostic, updatable, and intentionally written in plain, flexible language.

Which AI should I use for these prompts?

Use whatever AI assistant you have access to — the prompts adapt automatically.

Insider guidance:

- **ChatGPT** → best for structure, analysis, checklists
- **Claude** → best for nuance, tone, and interpretation
- **Gemini** → best for research and freshness
- **Grok** → best for trends, speed, and real-time shifts

Everything is written so you can **paste, edit, or narrate** without any special formatting or coding.

The New Literacy of Leadership

Artificial intelligence will not replace human judgment — it **multiplies** it.

In cybersecurity, where jargon often hides truth, leaders gain unfair advantage by asking sharper, cleaner questions.
This chapter turns that ability into a **living prompt library** you can update forever.

Every prompt:

- Works for executives, founders, MSPs, consultants, and vendors
- Can be run by voice ("Hey AI, run this prompt...")
- Includes a **real-world example**
- Shows an **Outcome Preview** so you know what good output looks like
- Allows simple replacement of bracketed variables:

[industry] [vendor] [contract excerpt] [system] [risk scenario]

Safety Box — How to Use AI Without Leaking Anything

1. **Never paste secrets, credentials, or incident evidence** into public models.
2. Prefer **enterprise, on-prem, air-gapped, or redacted versions**.
3. Maintain a **private Decision Log** for:

    - who asked
    - what question
    - which model
    - what decision it influenced

4. Treat AI outputs as **drafts** — you are the final reviewer.
5. When unsure, run prompts on **synthetic or anonymized inputs** first.

How to Use These Adaptive Prompts

1. Pick the scenario that fits your need.
2. Replace the bracketed variables with your details.
3. Narrate or paste into your secure AI workspace.
4. Read the output like a memo from your sharpest colleague.
5. Apply judgment before action.
6. If the output feels off — ask the AI what *inputs are missing*, then re-run it.
7. Save good prompts in a **Prompt Library Folder** so your team can reuse them.

SECTION 1 — Vendor Evaluation: From Promises to Proof

Prompt 1 — Adaptive Vendor Transparency Audit (Voice-ready)

"Act as an independent cybersecurity advisor for a [industry/organization].
Review this [vendor proposal or contract excerpt].
Identify undefined terms, unverified claims, and any section where jargon or ego reduces clarity.
List each as Claim → Verification Needed → Questions to Ask."

Example:
A hospital runs this on a SOC proposal; six phrases like "industry-grade response time" are flagged.

Outcome Preview:
A 1-page proof checklist emerges; the CIO enters negotiation with targeted questions.
Two claims are withdrawn, one rewritten with hard numbers.

Prompt 2 — Clarity Matrix Score (Future-Proof Diagnostic)

*"Using the Clarity Matrix — (Transparency × Competence ×
Consistency) ÷ Ego-Bias — score this [vendor/proposal] from 1–5
in each dimension.
Quote evidence for each score.
List what must be verified in writing before signing."*

Example:
A fintech startup compares three MSSPs.

Outcome Preview:
The ego-heavy vendor scores 13 and is removed; projected savings:
$60,000/year.

SECTION 2 — Contracts & Negotiation: Precision Over Panic

Prompt 3 — The "Promptly" Clause Scanner

*"Scan this [contract/proposal] for subjective language like
'promptly,' 'reasonable,' 'industry standard,' or 'best effort.'
Propose precise replacements with numbers and timeframes that
match modern cyber SLAs."*

Example:
"Respond promptly" → "Acknowledge P1 within 15 minutes;
contain within 4 hours."

Outcome Preview:
Ambiguity evaporates. Disputes die before they start.

Prompt 4 — Five-Lever Negotiation Coach

"Act as my procurement strategist.
Evaluate this [proposal/quote] using the five levers: Scope, Service
Levels, Data Ownership, Exit, Accountability.
For each lever, give three questions that turn vague promises into
measurable commitments."

Example:
Retailer discovers no log-export rights.

Outcome Preview:
New clause grants 24-hour log access. Leverage increases.

SECTION 3 — Crisis & Incident Response: Minutes That Matter

Prompt 5 — 60-Minute Ransomware Drill

"Simulate a ransomware event for a [org size + industry].
Generate a minute-by-minute plan for the first hour: actions,
contacts, artifacts, and executive updates."

Example:
Clinic discovers missing on-call contacts.

Outcome Preview:
A complete playbook drafted in an afternoon — before a real crisis.

Prompt 6 — Executive Brief Compressor

"Condense this [technical report] into a 200-word board brief:
impact, cause, cost, remediation, next steps."

Example:
12-page SOC report → 2-minute read.

Outcome Preview:
Backups budget approved instantly.

SECTION 4 — Compliance & Governance: Audits That Explain Themselves

Prompt 7 — Continuous Compliance Mapper

"Map these controls [HIPAA/SOC2/GDPR/ISO27001] to our systems.
Identify overlaps, gaps, and automation opportunities for evidence."

Example:
HIPAA logs satisfy half of SOC 2.

Outcome Preview:
Audit hours drop 40%.

Prompt 8 — Policy Translator for Humans

"Rewrite this [policy] so a manager can explain it in 60 seconds — accurate, plain, relatable."

Example:
"MFA required…" → "Always use a second step — a code, key, or biometric — for sensitive logins."

Outcome Preview:
Compliance rises, training time falls.

SECTION 5 — AI & Ethics: Machine Judgment with a Conscience

Prompt 9 — AI Risk Mirror

"Audit this [AI system].
List actions taken without human review.
Rate each by Impact, Reversibility, Explainability (1–5).
Recommend human-in-the-loop points."

Example:
Bank learns their AI auto-closes alerts.

Outcome Preview:
False negatives cut 70%.

Prompt 10 — Ethical Impact Lens

"Apply the five I's — Intent, Impact, Integrity, Interpretation,
Iteration — to this [AI use case].
State who benefits, who risks harm, and one mitigation per risk."

Example:
MSSP identifies bias favoring large clients.

Outcome Preview:
Transparent model becomes a marketing asset.

SECTION 6 — Board & Leadership: Turning Metrics Into Meaning

Prompt 11 — Quarterly Clarity Report Generator

"Using [MTTD, MTTR, Patch Rate, Awareness Score, Trust ROI], write a plain-language executive summary with trends and three next-quarter actions."

Example:
Detection time: 21 → 14 minutes.

Outcome Preview:
Board sees cyber as business, not tech.

Prompt 12 — Security Story Coach

"Turn this [incident or lesson] into a 2-minute clarity story with one measurable takeaway."

Example:
False alarm becomes a training success.

Outcome Preview:
CEO uses it at town hall.

SECTION 7 — Continuous Improvement: Make Clarity a Habit

Prompt 13 — Post-Incident Reflection Coach

"For Detection, Containment, and Recovery: What worked? What failed? What confused us? What taught us?
Suggest one metric for next quarter."

Outcome Preview:

Unified logs → response time halved.

Prompt 14 — 90-Day Clarity Plan Builder

"Design a 3-month clarity plan linking each Matrix dimension to one activity and KPI, with weekly check-ins."

SECTION 8 — Practical Guidelines for All Users

- **Protect data**: redact or synthesize
- **AI = advisor, not arbiter**
- **Keep a Prompt Journal**
- **Review quarterly**
- **Ask AI what inputs are missing**
- **Re-run improved prompts**

Meta-Prompt — The Universal Clarity Architect

"You are an AI Clarity Architect.
Given [my scenario], identify what is unclear and why it matters.
Write one measurable clarity question and the artifact needed to answer it.
Summarize the decision in one sentence a board can understand."

Outcome Preview:

Confusion → clarity → decision.

Closing Reflection

Prompts are mirrors.

They don't automate thinking — they expose assumptions and accelerate proof.

In a world where tools change weekly, **clarity is the habit that outlasts everything.**

Clarity isn't luck. It's language used on purpose.

BONUS Chapter 2 — The AI Decision Accelerator

How to Think With AI Before the Crisis Happens (Optional for Advanced Readers)

You can narrate every prompt in this chapter aloud — no typing required.
AI understands conversational decision-making just as well as text.

Most leaders use AI like a search box.
The ones who outperform everyone else use AI as a **decision simulator** — a place to rehearse high-stakes choices before the real world demands them.

This chapter teaches a **futureproof mental model** for thinking with AI.
No hype.
No technical deep dives.
Just replicable clarity.

---

1. Simulate Hard Decisions Before They Cost Money

Instead of asking AI for an answer, **teach it your constraints** first.

Voice-Ready Prompt

"You are helping us prepare for a major decision. Compare renewing Vendor A (stable, higher cost) with switching to Vendor B (cheaper, unproven).
Evaluate each using: clarity, reliability, resilience, long-term risk exposure, and total cost of confusion."

Why this works

You're not outsourcing judgment — you're **creating a second brain to compare your reasoning against**.

Pro move:

Score the AI's output with your Clarity Matrix.
    You'll see instantly where emotion, bias, or wishful thinking exists.

---

2. Transform Risk Plans Into Simple If/Then Scenarios

AI turns static risk documents into **living branches of possibility**.

Tell your AI:

"If this happens → then show me the next three steps, the evidence required, and the decision gate that follows."

Examples:

- If a vendor misses the SLA three times → map negotiation and exit pathway.
- If an incident triggers regulatory thresholds → draft insurer/legal/internal notices.
- If downtime > 2 hours → quantify financial, operational, and reputational impact.

Why it matters

Every If/Then run clarifies your organization's:

- risk tolerance
- response speed
- blind spots
- operational bottlenecks

AI becomes a **mirror**, not a crutch.

---

3. Use Multiple AI Systems to Cross-Check Thinking

Different AIs = different cognitive styles.

Instead of memorizing brand names, memorize **the pattern**:

- **Model Type 1 — Structurer**
  Organizes, clarifies, and analyzes.
- **Model Type 2 — Contextualizer**
  Spots nuance, ethics, tone, hidden assumptions.
- **Model Type 3 — Explorer**
  Provides research, patterns, and trend signals.

Rule of Thumb

When **two models agree**, confidence increases.
  When they **disagree**, clarity increases.

AI disagreement is not danger — it's a **diagnostic tool**.

---

4. Build Your AI Governance Routine (Lightweight + Practical)

Treat AI as a trusted advisor under NDA:
  helpful, quick, structured — but never the final authority.

Save three things in your AI Decision Log:

1. **Prompt used**
2. **AI's reasoning summary**
3. **Your final human decision + why**

This creates:

- audit transparency
- leadership clarity
- reduced cognitive drift
- better future decisions

It's not bureaucracy.
  It's **thinking with receipts**.

---

5. The 3-Minute Reflection Rule

Before accepting any AI recommendation, ask:

1. **What evidence supports this?**
2. **What assumption hides inside it?**
3. **What is the cost if it's wrong?**

This tiny pause turns AI from a "fast answer machine" into a **clarity amplifier**.

---

6. The Universal Meta-Prompt (Use Anywhere)

"Given this decision: [describe scenario],
  identify the real question behind the question,
  list the assumptions,
  show the clarity gap,
  and propose the smallest test that would change the decision."

This is the **AI equivalent of a flashlight in a dark room**.

---

7. When *Not* to Use AI

AI is NOT the right tool if:

- you're panicked
- you're dealing with unredacted sensitive data
- a human conversation is required
- the situation demands intuition, ethics, or HR boundaries

AI sharpens judgment — it should not be used in situations where **judgment itself is the risk**.

Final Insight

AI won't replace your judgment —
  but it will **magnify whatever judgment you bring to it**.

Leaders who learn to **coach** AI will outperform those who merely **consult** it.

Use this chapter as your starting point.
  Treat AI not as a mirror that flatters you —
  but one that **clarifies you**.
  And clarity is the real competitive advantage in an uncertain world.

Epilogue — The Clarity Manifesto

For Every Leader Who Chooses Understanding Over Fear

Epilogue — The Clarity Manifesto
For Every Leader Who Chooses Understanding Over Fear

- Clarity is not a luxury in the digital age—it's the oxygen of trust.
- We built firewalls but neglected conversations.
  We passed audits but skipped rehearsals.
  We automated protection but forgot reflection.
- This book has argued one idea from many angles:
  Cybersecurity is not a war between machines.
  It is a discipline of minds.
- Every framework you've read—from The Trust Gap to The Quantum Horizon—comes back to a single truth:
  You cannot secure what you do not understand, and you cannot lead what you do not question.

The Three Laws of Clarity

- **1. Transparency creates strength.**
  Secrets belong in encryption, not leadership.
  The clearer the process, the fewer the failures.
- **2. Precision inspires confidence.**
  Define everything—recovery windows, vendor duties, metrics, boundaries.
  The gap between *"promptly"* and *"15 minutes"* is the gap between blame and certainty.
- **3. Adaptation is survival.**
  In technology, permanence equals extinction.
  Security evolves only when leaders evolve.

The Human Equation

- Machines can accelerate work, but they cannot supply integrity.
  Compliance can organize behavior, but it cannot generate

courage.
AI can detect patterns, but it cannot practice humility.
- Cyber resilience always begins in character—in the quiet habit of asking:
"Is this clear? Is this fair? Is this tested?"
- The strongest organizations are built by leaders who value curiosity as much as control.

The Future We Deserve
- If the last century was defined by secrecy, this one must be defined by clarity.
- Nations, companies, and individuals will either cooperate through verified truth—or collapse under unverified confidence.
- The future of cybersecurity is not unbreakability.
It is *understandability*—systems that are transparent, predictable, testable, and resilient, even in failure.

A Leader's Promise to Their Organization
(Replaces the Oath — same meaning, professional tone)
A leader committed to clarity embraces six practices:
- choosing explanation over obscurity,
- measuring what matters,
- verifying before trusting,
- automating with boundaries,
- learning faster than the threat evolves,
- protecting dignity alongside data.

These practices are not ceremonial—they are operational.

Closing Perspective
- The next generation of cybersecurity leaders will not be defined by acronyms, but by the clarity they bring during uncertainty.
- If there is one message worth reinforcing, it is this:
The future is not defended by firewalls. It is defended by understanding.

Before Buying Cybersecurity: Think Securely. Choose Wisely.
Nikolay Gul

Sources & Further Reading

- **IBM Cyber Resilience Report (2024–2025)**
  https://www.ibm.com/reports/cyber-resilience-report
- **World Economic Forum — Global Risk Report**
  https://www.weforum.org/reports/global-risks-report-2025
- **ENISA Threat Landscape 2025**
  https://www.enisa.europa.eu/publications/enisa-threat-landscape-2025
- **Gartner Cybersecurity Forecast (2025)**
  https://www.gartner.com/en/documents/cybersecurity-trends-2025
- **MIT AI Ethics Lab — 2035 Projection Report**
  https://aiethics.mit.edu/reports/2035-forecast
- **NIST Post-Quantum Cryptography Program (2024–ongoing)**
  https://csrc.nist.gov/projects/post-quantum-cryptography
- **Allianz Risk Barometer 2025 (Cyber #1 Global Risk)**
  https://www.agcs.allianz.com/news-and-insights/reports/allianz-risk-barometer.html
- **CISA (US Cybersecurity & Infrastructure Security Agency) – Annual Threat Assessment**
  https://www.cisa.gov/resources-tools/resources/annual-threat-assessments
- **CISA Zero Trust Maturity Model (2024)**
  https://www.cisa.gov/zero-trust-maturity-model
- **NIST Supply Chain Risk Management Framework**
  https://csrc.nist.gov/projects/supply-chain-risk-management

Acknowledgments

To my wife - thank you for being my most trusted network, my constant uptime, and the only person with full admin rights to my heart.
You kept the system online when the author definitely bluescreened, patched my logic when it leaked, and rebooted my sanity more than once. You've proven, conclusively, that love is still the most secure connection on the planet.
Nothing in this book exists without your patience, humor, and the way you reminded me (gently… and sometimes not so gently) to eat, sleep, and touch grass.

To the cybersecurity professionals who spend sleepless nights defending networks most people never think about—this book is for you. Your vigilance powers the world's digital heartbeat, often without applause. Thank you for holding the line.

To the collaborators across AI, cybersecurity, and publishing including Claude, Gemini, Grok, and the GPT system that endured my endless revisions—thank you for challenging every idea until it could defend itself. This project is sharper because you sharpened me.

To the readers, founders, consultants, and entrepreneurs who shared real stories of confusion, loss, recovery, and resilience your experiences kept this book grounded in the real world. You turned theories into practical tools and made every chapter better.

And to everyone who believes clarity is more powerful than fear: thank you for building a future where people can make smarter decisions without needing a translator.

About the Author

Nikolay Gul is an author, strategist, and AI-driven marketing and cybersecurity advisor focused on closing the gap between advanced technology and everyday human understanding.

His **AI-Enhanced Clarity Models** blend technical depth with practical simplicity, turning complexity into decisions people can actually use.

He is the founder of **Future-Proof Marketing Press**, a publishing imprint dedicated to making security, AI, and innovation understandable for non-technical decision-makers in an age defined by noise, complexity, and accelerating change.

He is the author of several well-received books, including:

- *The 19 Laws of AI Prompting Intelligence*
- *AI-Driven Cybersecurity & High-Tech Marketing*
- *AI Time Machine – The Art of Prompting*
- *Easy Book Self-Publishing: A Step-by-Step Guide With AI Assistance*

Nikolay Gul Profile: linkedin.com/in/webdesignerny/
Amazon Author Page: amazon.com/s?k=nikolay+gul
Barnes & Noble Author Page: barnesandnoble.com/s/nikolay+gul

* 9 7 9 8 9 9 2 7 4 4 0 9 5 *